W9-CYC-303

Individual and Group Therapy

COMBINING PSYCHOANALYTIC TREATMENTS

INDIVIDUAL
AND
GROUP THERAPY

Combining Psychoanalytic Treatments

JUDITH CALIGOR

NINA D. FIELDSTEEL

ALBERT J. BROK

Basic Books, Inc., Publishers   *New York*

Library of Congress Cataloging in Publication Data

Caligor, Judith.
    Individual and group therapy.

    References
    Includes index.
    1. Psychoanalysis.   2. Group psychoanalysis.   I. Field-
steel, Nina D.   II. Brok, Albert J.   III. Title.
[DNLM: 1. Psychoanalytic Therapy—methods.   2. Psycho-
therapy, Group.   WM 430 C153i]
RC506.C25   1984   616.89'17   83–46117
ISBN   0–465–03250–8

For Asya Kadis,
an Inspired Teacher
and an Exceptional Woman

CONTENTS

Contents

FOREWORD

This volume is the first to provide a full and well-organized account on the subject of combining individual and group psychoanalytic psychotherapy. It incorporates material provided by a scattering of articles published forty years ago by such authors as Helen Durkin, Henriette Glatzer, Asya Kadis, Edrita Fried, Toby and Irving Bieber, and others. It also adds significantly to the more numerous articles published in the fifties and sixties.

Because of their extensive experience during the seventies in combining individual and group analytic therapy, the authors have been able to provide us with a great deal of pertinent and very specific information, as well as with illuminating illustrations about each step of the process. Although they define their particular method (described in chapter 1) as "combined analytic therapy," they point out that as late as 1976 the basic principles used by most therapists were the same, in spite of the fact that some of them applied different techniques or methods of executing these principles.

The authors endorse psychoanalysis as the soundest method of treatment and describe variations among analysts, like those between Heinz Kohut and Robert Searles. They also point out the limitations of psychoanalysis and summarize the conditions that led to the increasing use of group therapy and eventually of combined individual and group psychotherapy. Finally, they provide specific information on every aspect of the therapists' tasks: their decision whether or not to use combined treatment; how they help the patient and the group to make the transition from individual to group therapy; their own experience and countertransferential interactions; and the impact of the group process on transference, on the self-image of the patients, on working through, on their use of dreams, and on just how termination is to be carried out.

Whether the reader employs analytic or some other form of combined therapy, and even if he or she is not interested in it at all, I believe that the authors' clinical expertise will prove to be of eminent practical value.

HELEN E. DURKIN, Ph.D.

PREFACE

This book is for therapists trained in individual analytic therapy who have started, or would like to start, a group made up of their analytic patients.

Although psychoanalysts have been combining individual and group therapy for at least forty years, their clinical observations and theoretical formulations have not been presented in an integrated form. Certain truths seem to be affirmed again and again. Our own experiences and observations have been consistent with the findings of other clinicians.

We have attempted here to develop the body of knowledge that does exist by integrating the literature and our own clinical experience, and relating it to contemporary theories in the practice of psychoanalytic therapy.

The current model for combined analytic therapy—in which the patient is in individual and group treatment with the same therapist—has developed over the years from the interplay of theoretical formulations and clinical experience. Clinical concerns, the patients' needs, and their reports of what has been therapeutically useful have all contributed to our current practice, which we will present here.

Reviewing our own work in recent years, we start with the

premise that clinical experience takes primary importance. We have tried to integrate this with our theoretical understandings. Since we feel that our work with patients has been a vivid and compelling source of increasing our understanding of both theory and technique, we have included detailed clinical case examples. The clinical validation of theoretical constructs provides a vitality essential to effective therapeutic work. We thank our patients for all they have taught us.

Combined analytic therapy confronts the task of psycho-analysis—the development of insight—through the analysis of transference and resistance, through developing an under-standing of the genetic origins of current concerns, and through the vicissitudes of the working-through process. Adding group to the individual treatment allows the power of group therapy to enhance the total treatment and is particularly effec-tive in amplifying and clarifying some of the difficulties of the working-through phase of therapy.

The other approach to adding group therapy to individual analytic treatment was presented by Louis Ormont and Her-bert Strean (1978). In their model of conjoint therapy the patient is in individual analytic treatment with one therapist and in group therapy with another. Our conviction that the therapeutic relationship is the core of the analytic process of growth leads us, in most cases, to question this recommenda-tion. The uniqueness of the patient-therapist relationship and the construction of a meaningful life story within this context (Dyrud 1980; Schafer 1983; Spence 1982) cannot easily be extended into a relationship with an additional therapist. From our perspective it is likely that this form of added group therapy will conflict with, rather than enhance, the developing psy-choanalytic process. The new experience that group would provide might better be obtained in life situations encouraged by and understood in the individual treatment if combined treatment is not available or is contraindicated.

Other models of group therapy are concerned with developing self-awareness. There are group therapies which focus only on interactions and interrelations within the group. Others are primarily problem-centered and may or may not be time-limited. Some group therapists use action techniques to promote interaction and heighten self-awareness. To some extent each of these approaches to group has demonstrated its effectiveness. We have used what we have learned from each of these in the working-through phase to the extent that such techniques promote the individual analytic process.

There are other curative factors implicit in the group experience that derive from other theoretical models. Humanistic and existential thinking have made their contributions to therapy. Many varieties of experiences promote growth and development. For example, in recent years we have seen the emergence of a wide range of self-help groups that have been extremely effective. Some have been led by trained group therapists; others have been described as leaderless groups. They have been centered on particular life problems, such as alcoholism, widowhood, or cancer, or on certain existential problems, as in women's consciousness-raising groups. It may be a reflection of the particular and unique stresses of our culture that there has been an increasing move to find solutions to problems in a group context. There is a demonstrated need for the strengths and the amplifications of experience provided by the group setting.

We have addressed this book to psychoanalysts interested in working in group therapy with their analytic patients. We would hope that by our careful discussion of some of the complex issues in this type of therapy we have made it clear that additional training is desirable. Along with reading the related literature, research, and theory, training in group therapy requires experience in group. We have discussed the importance for therapists to have some experience in a group to heighten their own awareness of how they function in a group setting and how their behavior may differ from behavior in the one-to-one setting. We have also found that group supervision of one's work as a group therapist sharpens awareness of the transference and countertransference reactions in the group therapy work.

Training provides opportunities for further growth and development both as therapists and for us personally. We have each had the experience of finding that as we developed our skills as group therapists, there was a concomitant increase in our abilities to work more effectively with patients in individual therapy. Combining analytic treatments affects both patients and their therapists.

Throughout this book the case material is carefully disguised. As psychoanalysts, our first responsibility is to our patients. The privacy of the analytic session, individual and group, cannot be breached, since privacy and confidentiality are the essential elements that make it possible for the patient to put his trust in another human being. In portraying the group, we use composite units from groups led by or supervised by the authors, to prevent the uniqueness of any group from being recognized. We hope that these compromises will permit us to maintain the integrity of the individual psychodynamics, to focus on recurrent or specific group interactions, and at the same time maintain confidentiality for our patients.

ACKNOWLEDGMENTS

This book comes out of the unique experience of training and teaching in the Group Department of the Postgraduate Center for Mental Health in New York City. Asya Kadis, and later Marvin Aronson, created a training atmosphere there that has allowed analytic therapists to learn and exchange ideas with each other in a truly open climate. The senior faculty we learned from—Helen Durkin, Edrita Fried, Henrietta Glatzer, and Alexander Wolf—were talented and original therapists, each creative in their own ways. Their experience, communicated to us, was the groundwork for this book.

We also want to thank our patients and students for constantly teaching us and illuminating the process in which we are collaboratively engaged. Special thanks to our spouses who have been patient and helpful throughout the work on this book, and to our children for their patience and understanding. We wish particularly to thank Lee Caligor for his careful reading of the manuscript and his thoughtful, professional comments.

We consistently appreciated our editor, Jo Ann Miller, for her remarkable ability to enable us to say what we wanted in ways that communicated. Her criticism always managed to be constructive and made it possible for us to develop the manuscript to its present form. We add our thanks to Joanne Kirtland for her ability to order and clarify as she typed the manuscript.

JUDITH CALIGOR
NINA D. FIELDSTEEL
ALBERT J. BROK

Individual and Group Therapy

COMBINING PSYCHOANALYTIC TREATMENTS

CHAPTER 1

Combining Individual and Group Therapy: Definition and Rationale

K ATE came into the room for her first group therapy session visibly annoyed that someone was sitting in what she thought of as her place. She was scowling, her classic Latin beauty and natural grace marred by the anger that radiated from her. She had been determined not to greet the new group as she greeted every other situation, hoping she would not hide behind what she called "the shrew." One of the themes in Kate's individual therapy had been the fear of rejection as she had experienced it within her family and her abrasive defense against that fear, which elicited the very reaction she dreaded. Kate insisted that she was aptly named for Shakespeare's famous shrew.

The ensuing group session made Kate edgy. To Eric's talk of "the girls in the office," Kate snapped, "Do you get the coffee?" To Estelle's talk about her children and mention of her weekend house, Kate muttered under her breath about "pampered children" and "self-indulgent life styles." As Sam talked about his fights with his wife, she challenged, "You're a coward. Why don't you just fight back?"

In her individual session the following day Kate cried; she had been sure no one would like her, so "the shrew" had emerged to defend her. Now the therapist, too, knew what she was really like. The defensive aspect of her behavior evoked by the group had never been so vividly demonstrated within the constraints of the one-to-one relationship of individual therapy. Kate was sure that no one in the group would know that she had really been very frightened.

Though Kate could use her sharp, aggressive style success-fully in her work in the advertising world, she always felt unloved and unlovable in her personal relationships. In her individual therapy she had come to understand how she re-peated her early history again and again, first reexperiencing it and then eliciting it. Seeing her behavior played out in the group, noting her reactions to group members and theirs to her, allowed Kate to see what had been talked about in her individual therapy in a new context. Adding group therapy to her individual therapy would now help Kate work through her frightened and defensive responses as she integrated new un-derstanding of her behavior.

A Definition of Combined Therapy

In the therapy we are describing, patients are introduced to a group conducted by their individual analyst during the work-ing-through phase of the treatment. The experience in the group becomes an integral part of the treatment process. The unique strengths of group therapy amplify the total treatment process.

Patients begin in individual therapy, for it is here that the working alliance can be established, psychodynamic understandings can be developed, and the origins of their behavior in their unique history can be explored. Individual therapy provides a level of highly attuned individual relatedness not possible in groups, and most patients require an extended period of this. Adding the group experience to the individual analytic therapy, allows the working-through process to be more realized, insight to be translated into behavioral changes, and the entrenched characterological defenses to be modified. Combined individual and group therapy, in fact, amplifies the total therapy experience by providing more varied and differentiated relationships. The group promotes more complete individuation, enhances the development of a stable sense of self, and encourages a more independent, self-determined relationship with the therapist. It serves to more fully complete the developmental tasks to which analytic therapy addresses itself.

Historical Roots

We will better understand the rationale behind this type of therapy if we look at the context in which it developed.

The confluence of intellectual developments and social needs in the 1940s contributed to the rapid growth of group psychotherapy in general and of analytic group therapy in particular. As a result of the cataclysmic events in Europe, many prominent social psychologists and psychoanalysts emigrated to the United States. The psychoanalysts represented a wide variety of training, backgrounds, and approaches to psychoanalysis. The ideas of the émigrés merged with the tradition of pragmatism in psychiatry prevalent in the United States (Rosenbaum and Berger 1975). They broadened our definition of psychoanalytic treatment while widening acceptance of Freud's theories. At the same time, the active experimentation of social psychologists such as Kurt Lewin (1951), Fritz Heider (1958), and others (Cartwright and Zander 1968) focused on the patternings of interpersonal relations and the phenomenological field in which an event occurs.

Dating back to the early years of the century, educational and supportive groups had been used to treat patients with particular physical and psychological disorders. For example, Joseph Pratt, a New England physician, organized tuberculosis patients into groups for discussions and lectures in the hope of changing attitudes towards hygiene (1907). His approach yielded to various combinations of inspirational and psychoanalytically derived group methods during the 1930s (Rosenbaum and Berger 1975, 6).

During and after World War II, societal pressures stemming from the need to understand the development of the Nazi movement in Germany, as well as from the needs developing out of our own military efforts, spurred social psychologists to study group structure and group process. Kurt Lewin, who coined the term "group dynamics," was concerned with group formation and the effects of leadership styles. His work was influential in the development of our understanding of the relationship between the individual and the group and the use of the group in changing attitudes. He believed and sought to demonstrate that it was easier to change individuals formed into a group than to change any of them separately (Lewin 1947.) His experiments showed that attitudes and behavior could indeed be changed if they were examined, found unsatisfactory, and revised by group discussion. Derivations of his work led to understanding and identifying people's perceptions of their environmental context and the social forces maintaining it (Kelley 1967; Jones and Davis 1965).

Traditionally psychoanalysts had centered their attention on the strength of the unconscious processes that resisted change. But in the postwar years, different theoretical orientations stressing the social and interpersonal began to affect the practice of psychoanalysis. Traditional Freudian theory was being revised in many quarters by clinicians who were deeply impressed by the impact of social, cultural, and interpersonal variables (Kardiner 1939, 1945; Sullivan 1953; Horney 1953).

In the 1950s, interest in the use of analytic group therapy developed in response to two very different sets of problems. A broader segment of the population was seeking analytic treatment, many of whom could not pay for extended individual therapy several times a week. Perhaps more important, there was also an increasing awareness that there were patients in psychoanalytic treatment three, four, or even five times a week who were not really progressing, changing, or growing in their everyday life.

In the late 1940s and early 1950s, the Postgraduate Center for Mental Health, a clinic and training facility in New York City, provided the opportunity for psychoanalysts who were concerned with these issues and developing techniques of analytic therapy to meet and share their knowledge and experience. In the Group Department, established in 1954, psychoanalysts teaching and working began to report their experiments with different forms of combined individual and group therapies. Helen Durkin's *The Group in Depth* proposed that the patient's defensive maneuvers that did not evoke anxiety because they were ego-syntonic "were responsible for most of the technical difficulties which arise between analyst and patient" (1962, 140). Durkin felt that these maneuvers were more effectively addressed in the group as confrontations by peers were less threatening than from the therapist, yet were difficult to dismiss. The therapist and the group members were able to observe a person's acting out of unconscious conflicts in the group, which made the underlying issues more accessible to treatment.

In comparing individual therapy to group, the format of individual therapy was found to be particularly appropriate for achieving the major therapeutic aims of the initial phases of analytic treatment: forming a working relationship, training the patient to be a patient, motivating him towards further explorations of his personality, and providing a foundation of trust and confidence which would be indispensable later on when the anxiety which attends all personality reorganization emerges (Aronson 1979). This meant that group therapy was effective primarily in the later phases of treatment.

Toby Bieber (1971, 162) pointed out that the distinction some writers make between dyadic therapy as the setting for insight and the various group therapies as settings for interaction is a spurious one. She elaborated that reconstructive processes that transpire in each setting do not freeze within rigidly held boundaries, rather that there is reciprocal feedback. In general, she felt that the individual session is predominantly concerned with exploration of historical background and belief systems, while in the group attention is more centrally focused on the exposure and analysis of defenses.

Many variations of the timing and frequency of group and individual sessions were tried. The therapeutic stance of the therapist in the two settings was experimented with and stud-

ied. Increasingly it appeared that the effects of the two therapies when combined were not simply additive but complexly
interactive and could even cancel each other out. Alexander
Wolf and Emmanuel Schwartz, two of the analysts who first
wrote about analytic group therapy, mentioned combining the
therapies, indicating that it had not been helpful in their practices. "Ideally, one might think that such an arrangement
would be optimal; but in practice, combined therapy often
leads to a lessening of the effectiveness of both methods"
(1962, 180). Concerned with this issue, S. H. Foulkes and E.
James Anthony (1957) preferred sequential use of the two
modalities to avoid the negative effects of the interaction between them. Either group therapy should follow individual as
a "rounding off" process, or individual should be preceded by
group as a preparatory measure.

Other writers addressed themselves to the difficulties posed
by specific groups of patients and how combined treatment
provided the special considerations required. For example,
Edrita Fried's (1954) experience was that a combined model
of treatment reduced the number of passive-narcissistic patients who dropped out of treatment prematurely. The group
sessions provided a "unique situation for confronting the anxiety, defensiveness, and self-preoccupation behind the facade of
cooperation and charm" in these patients. Fried found the
combined therapy model permitted her to get beyond the
technical difficulty these patients presented because the narcissistic defenses were experienced as ego-syntonic. She also noted
that combined therapy was especially valuable in clarifying the
countertransference reactions these "personally charming"
people tend to evoke in a one-to-one situation.

David Schecter (1959) found that combined therapy was
particularly suitable for patients whose preadolescence had

been disturbed by defective or traumatic peer relationships. However, he specified that the infantile transference should be worked through in individual treatment before introducing the patient to the group. He felt that premature group therapy only solidified defenses against exposing and resolving infantile dynamics.

The profusion of papers in the 1950s and the 1960s on combining group and individual analytic therapies was followed by a period of less published debate and discussion. Over the years at the Postgraduate Center Group Department, there continued to be interest in the various approaches to analytic group therapy. In a 1976 conference some of the faculty presented their clinical experience in combining the two modalities. It is of note that faculty members reported remarkably similar clinical experience. Most preferred dyadic treatment for the first phase of the treatment, and continued it in combination with the group at the later stages. All the therapists confirmed the complexity of the interaction of the two modalities and the effects on the transference and on the manifestations of resistance (Aronson et al. 1976).

An Overview of the Psychoanalytic Approach

The term "psychoanalytic therapy" covers a broad range of therapeutic practices that reflect basic differences in assumptions and expectations. For this reason it is useful to present an overview of our clinical generalizations and of the psychoanalytic concepts we find the most clarifying and explanatory of the clinical experiences.

We are talking about a group of patients who go into psychoanalytic treatment two or three times a week for an extended period. We do not draw a sharp distinction between psychoanalysis and psychotherapy, following John Gedo's formulations that every patient brings to the therapy problems from each subphase within the developmental hierarchy which vary in proportion depending on the exact nature of the personality (1981). That is to say, in our language, that patients come to treatment presenting a complex picture resulting from their reactions to early developmental experiences, to the evolution of their competence or mastery, to the sexual identifications that emerge from the unique constellations of their families, and to their present life situations.

Individual histories vary infinitely. Despite infantile residuals, intense physical anxiety, or oral cravings, some people can manage a competent, responsible work life and show early imprints only in their emotionally and sexually intimate relationships. Others function well socially and sexually when protected by a supportive relationship, but cannot function competently in the competitive work world. The first phase of combined treatment, involving only individual sessions, provides the opportunity to address the particular needs of each patient in his or her areas of greatest deficit.

Throughout the treatment process patients' therapeutic needs vary in response to the treatment situation and to their ongoing life. As treatment progresses, there is less of the earlier need for modulation and integration and more for conflict definition and resolution, but for most patients some fluctuation between the two persists. In Stolorow and Lachman's words (1980, 174), "The therapeutic relationship may shift back and forth between the more advanced and the more primitive positions throughout the analysis. The progressive and regressive shifts occur as the patient's psychopathology unfolds and is met with the required empathy and skillful interpretations. The two levels of object relations may coexist." When patients feel particularly helpless and diffuse, they require primarily support and empathy in the response; when they feel stronger, clearly separate and involved with their inner conflicts, interventions that address the conflict are most valuable.

It is the total situation for the patient at a particular moment in time that will determine the therapeutic intervention or recommendation. The therapist decides what will be most productive for change while permitting the patient to maintain the level of functioning required to continue his ongoing life. In the course of treatment this will involve interventions that are verbal or nonverbal, with differing emphases on the empathic, educative, or interpretive. The patient may be lying on the couch or sitting up facing the therapist. At some points the patient's needs for relatedness and contact will be best served by sitting in a position where he can see the therapist. At other times access needed to less conscious, solitary experience requires less reassuring, more regressive conditions and is best reached by the patient lying on the couch with the therapist out of visual range. The therapist decides on each of these, gearing his judgment toward effecting the most profound and widespread improvement in self-awareness and functioning possible for each patient.

Central to the entire psychoanalytic process is what Schafer describes in *The Analytic Attitude* (1983). Here he spells out lucidly and sensibly the true significance of analytic neutrality as a stance permitting optimal growth in psychoanalytic treatment:

> In maintaining the analytic attitude, the analyst confronts, clarifies, and interprets these seductive strategies in a funda-

mentally neutral manner, thereby paving the way toward the analysand's believing that it may be safe to become a whole person engaged with whole others. In other words the analysand becomes readier to experience and contain the tension of opposities within a unified self-presentation, however painfully this may be done (60).

This does not preclude human relatedness or perceptiveness, but does discourage the analyst from taking a position that is judgmental or presumptuous.

Initiating Treatment

People usually seek therapy in response to a crisis. Unhappy life situations, a disappointing love affair, a frustrating job, a troubled marriage, or problems with children or parents generate anxiety and intolerable discomfort and move the person to seek treatment. The patient often feels that this external situation is the crux of the problem and relies on the therapist to determine what form the help should take and how the therapy should proceed. Most people are in therapy for some time before they understand what they really want to change. They enter therapy simply wanting relief from discomfort and stress. The following examples are typical of therapy beginnings.

Joan's lover had given her an ultimatum: unless she would make a commitment to marriage, he would not continue in the relationship. Joan felt anxious and pressured by his request and came to therapy because she could not make a decision. The therapist began to explore Joan's history with her. Childhood experiences had created a high level of anxiety and an inability to trust others that had reappeared in each subsequent relationship at the point when she needed to make a commitment. It was clear both to the patient and to the therapist that the decision she was being pressed to make needed to be made. It was also clear that it could not be made wisely until she better understood her tremendous difficulty trusting men and the profound rage that erupted in relationships with them.

Robert came to therapy "surprised" that his last mistress had left him—usually he left, to return to his wife. Successive affairs had not helped free him from his unhappy marriage, and with each episode he felt more guilty and less able to make changes. The same pattern of crises was repeated in his business life. His successful business was run so as to repeatedly court disaster. He would then boldly rescue everything by a daring maneuver or brilliant innovation. In the course of exploration, it became clear to the analyst that the successive crises with his mistress and his business were an acting out of unconscious conflicts and involved Robert's defense against overwhelming feelings of impotence and rage. It would be necessary for the meaning of the drama to be understood if this repetitive pattern was to be successfully interrupted.

An initial consultation may last for several sessions so that the therapist can form an impression of the person and some sense of the implications of the problems he or she brings to therapy. In Joan's case, accounts of intensely disorganizing anxiety under stress in her present life seemed related to her story of family life, which had been violently disrupted by World War II creating a loss of equilibrium in her early caretaking. With Robert, further exploration revealed that narcissistic wounds early in life had led to a defensive structure in which he repeatedly had to brilliantly and dramatically demonstrate his adequacy and potency.

During the first sessions the therapist usually makes tentative decisions about the recommended course of therapy and gives the patient information about time, fees, and plans for procedure. In most cases, the patient relies on the therapist to determine what is the best course of treatment. The subject of combined therapy, of adding group therapy after a period of individual treatment, may or may not come up in the individual consultation. It depends on the questions the patient raises and on the therapist's impression of what the most effective treatment plan might be for the particular patient. Because the choice of combined therapy for a patient is based on the clinical information that emerges in therapy, the therapist may decide not to address it at all at this early stage.

The Individual Therapy

The core of therapy, the relationship between the patient and the therapist, begins in the consultation process and evolves during the treatment. Two constructs conceptualize the important aspects of this relationship: the working alliance and the transference. Transference and the working alliance are conceptualized as separate entities even though they do not evidence themselves as discrete; rather, all interactions with the therapist have aspects of each. Transference denotes the idiosyncratic distortions which are the vehicles for the patient's past experience and perceptions that come into the therapy session. Transference covers the whole range of feelings, attitudes, and fantasies toward the analyst that originate in regard to significant persons of early childhood (Greenson 1967). The working alliance denotes the actual collaboration of patient and therapist.

It is in the context of the working alliance that the patient learns to be an analytic patient. He or she begins to report thoughts and experiences within the session and in private life, to trace present reactions to their origins in the past, to remember and report dreams, and to collaboratively explore all aspects of experience.

As part of this collaborative effort, the patient learns to talk about reactions to the therapist, feelings that are being evoked, and fantasies that have been set off. From these, and from the patient's manner of interacting with the therapist, the transference reactions become evident, the part that the patient's idiosyncratic past contributes to the situation. Gradually the patient becomes aware of bringing aspects of early experience to the present interaction with the therapist and begins to learn about previously unrecognized aspects of his or herself.

As time goes on, the patient develops a view of his or her own history, a result of recollections and the therapist's comments and interpretations. Together the patient and therapist evolve a construction regarding the patient's past—they develop a "particular story line." Jarl Dyrud, discussing Roy Schafer and Harry Stack Sullivan, points out that both describe psychotherapy as "a process of getting help from an expert in making some necessary revisions in a morbid story line" (1980, 335). As in all therapy, this story line will be continuously revised in the course of combined therapy, but it is formulated in the individual phase.

We see this revision of the life story most clearly in the patient's view of his or her parents. Amy, for example, first presented her mother as a murderously destructive, sadistic, and uncaring woman. Reexperiencing some early events and coming to understand some more recent ones, Amy was able to recognize that her mother's rages and frustrations in the past had imprinted themselves on her so indelibly that she had been unable to establish an appropriate rational relationship with the more reasonable aspects of her mother. She began to see that her defensive standoffishness in the present was masking a terror of contact and a tremendous fear of how hurt she would be if she permitted herself to get closer to others.

In this way, the patient begins to understand the more obvious relationships between current difficulties and her life story. Amy's therapist was aware that it was important for Amy to face her during the sessions. She was aware that Amy responded to every nuance in her facial expression. An open and trusting relationship with the therapist was an opportunity for Amy to try out something different and then to try extending it into her life. As reactions from others to her increased openness provided increased satisfactions, Amy was able to utilize her expanding insights for further change.

As treatment progresses, negative transferences emerge and are dealt with. The crucial importance of working with these negative transferences was first pointed out by Freud, and was reemphasized by Ralph Greenson as being an extremely productive aspect of analytic work, given the presence of a good working alliance. The reliving of experience in the transference of hostility and hatred to the early childhood figures carries great impact (Greenson 1967, 235). Most frequently indications of negative feelings of the patient toward the therapist first surface in nonverbal behavior, in slips, and in dreams. Susan, for example, had frequent dreams of intrusive figures, customs agents, or repressive teachers, whom she reacted to by withdrawing. She was gradually able to see the relationship between this and the rather distant, excessively accommodating, and undemanding behavior she insisted on maintaining in the relationship with her therapist. She was also able to recall a persistent childhood feeling that she was a bother to her mother, that it would be best to make no demands if she wanted to avoid evoking tremendous rage from her mother.

A new emphasis on the particular importance of the relationship between patient and therapist in effecting change has been the focus of much of the current writing in psychoanalysis. Freud and other early writers stressed the importance of the analysis of the transference as the pathway to insight and cure. Kohut (1977), Modell (1976), and Searles (1979) stress that the therapeutic relationship itself is crucial to furthering the patient's development.

Harold Searles, in "Concerning Therapeutic Symbiosis," states:

> In psychoanalytic treatment, what is needed more than anything else to resolve a fixation in the patient's ego development, his having achieved what is only a fragment or fragments of an ego, is his discovery that a fellow human being, the analyst, can come to know and work with him.

He goes on to say,

> Just as we need to realize that in healthy human living symbiotic relatedness is not confined to infancy and early childhood, but forms at largely though not entirely unconscious levels the dynamic substrate of adult living, so too individuation is not a once and for all irreversible process (1979, 176–77).

Heinz Kohut addresses the same issue, extending these ideas to people in general, not just the disturbed patient. "The psychologically healthy adult continues to need the mirroring of the self by self-objects (to be exact, by the self-object aspects of his love objects), and he continues to need targets for his idealization. No implication of immaturity or psychopathology must therefore be derived from the fact that another person is used as a self-object. Self-object relations occur on all developmental levels and in psychological health as well as in psychological illness" (1977, 188).

These views reflect a growing awareness of the importance of relationship aspects of the treatment in therapeutic change. Reciprocally, the role of insight as the crucial instrument of change in psychoanalytic therapy has been modified and reduced. In *The Fallacy of Understanding*, Edgar Levenson (1972) addressed this issue. Expanding on Sullivan's concepts, he stresses that therapy occurs interpersonally though changes may occur intrapsychically. Stephen Appelbaum (1981) in a recent volume on effecting change, entitles his chapter on insight "The Idealization of Insight as an Enemy of Change," noting that insight is an important contributor to change, but that seeing it as the exclusive factor can obstruct important alternate pathways. Clearly, insight does not always lead to change.

As we move from viewing insight as the sole determinant of psychological change, the importance of sensitively maintaining and developing the relationship of the patient and the therapist increases. "If structural changes in the patient's personality mean anything, it must mean that we assume that ego development is resumed in the therapeutic process in psychoanalysis. And this resumption of ego development is contingent on a relationship with a new object, the analyst" (Loewald 1960, 16).

This crucial therapeutic relationship, established and developed in the individual treatment situation, is the core of the combined analytic therapy and remains central to the whole process of individual and group treatment. The understanding of the patient's life history, the comprehending of the therapeutic process and its gradual introduction of change are built on the relationship between patient and therapist.

Rationale for Adding Group to the Individual Analytic Therapy

Many patients who make substantial progress in the early stages of individual treatment later slow up, reaching impasses that do not move them to resolution. Subsequently some patients end treatment with more limited gains than they seem to have the potential for. Our hypotheses about the source of these limitations fall into two categories: the limits of dyadic analytic treatment in general; and the limits of any particular dyad.

The experience of the analyst as the trusted authority who permits the patient to feel safe, to trust, and to regress in the service of productive analyzing is crucial in the early stages of treatment. However, in some cases the treatment bogs down in the process of translating insight into change. Insight does not necessarily flow into changes in behavior. The analytic session, with sensitive listening and appreciation by the analyst, may not evoke the anxieties and the defenses stimulated by inattention, competition, or rivalry in everyday life. Although these issues are talked about and touched on in the transference, they are frequently not lived through in the individual sessions. The experience of patients (particularly when therapists become patients in group) testifies to this again and again. Susan, for example, had gradually become freer and more open in the course of her therapy, but continued to feel vast dissatisfaction in her personal relationships. For Susan, adding group to individual therapy provided an opportunity to have her therapist present as she encountered the bewildering repetitive experience of feeling disconnected and deadened.

Susan was an attractive woman in her thirties who had made considerable progress in twice-a-week analytic treatment. She had come to know herself better, move out into new situations, start a new career, and be increasingly open and direct in the working alliance. Negative transferences had surfaced and been acknowledged; her relationship with her mother, whom Susan felt had pushed her aside, ignored, and generally rejected her in childhood, had improved significantly and gratifyingly in the present. However, most of Susan's other relationships continued to be disappointing, rejecting, and unfulfilling.

Some months after starting in group, a clear pattern had emerged. Susan would be animated, responsive, and vital, as in her individual sessions, when the group focused on her specifically. But when they moved on to somebody else, she would abruptly go blank, as if she'd been switched off. Confronted by the group about this as it happened repeatedly, Susan was at first uncomprehending but gradually became aware of how automatically she disengaged from what was going on in group as the attention shifted from her.

Bill, a patient in the same group, saw in Susan's behavior a perfect reflection of his own experience and was able to understand something about himself that he could never tolerate before. In his empathic response to Susan when she was confronted by the group, he was able to examine his own defenses. A warm, connected feeling developed between Susan and Bill as both used their good sense of humor to talk about it admitting, "Of course the world stopped when the spotlight wasn't on me." They could share how terrible they felt at those moments, and how much a part of their existence it had been—they had never really been aware that it was different anywhere else, or for anybody else. In her individual sessions, Susan and her therapist were able to examine together what happened to her when she was not centered on empathically, how easily threatened she was, and how quick she was to resume narcissistic defenses.

Sharon benefited from the addition of group in a different way. In contrast to Susan, she was easily able to relate empathically with other people, but would become disorganized and enraged when differed with. When she entered treatment, Sharon had been severely depressed and hypersensitive to a nearly paranoid level. Over the years she had made substantial progress, including a marriage to a man she both loved and admired, and had gained the ability to work hard and consistently. During her individual sessions, when the therapist would suggest a possible difference from Sharon's perception of reality, Sharon responded with tears and sullenness, yet the therapeutic relationship would resume. However, it continued to be difficult for Sharon to tolerate this kind of confrontation in her relationship to others.

Soon after she entered the group, Sharon began to be emotionally generous to others, but with the implicit expectation that in return she would receive the kind of loving, sensitive attention she craved. Although this sometimes occurred, it was certainly not consistent. Each member of the group, in the context of his or her own defensive structures, responded unevenly and ambivalently. Sharon felt as she frequently did with her husband and family; she was always being disappointed. As she struggled with this in group, Sharon began for the first time to understand the impasse she had reached with her adolescent stepdaughter. Sharon expected reciprocation for her loving attention from the girl, but had no awareness of the girl's

22

adolescent struggles, which made reciprocation virtually impossible and undesirable.

Building on the relationship she had developed with her therapist in individual therapy, as well as on a certain level of integration of her defenses, increased her ability to understand and modulate her reactions. Sharon slowly learned to tolerate disagreements and disappointments without disorganizing or needing to obliterate the relationship.

Each patient and therapist has a unique relationship. Although it was once believed that treatment unfolded in the same fashion regardless of the therapist, it is now recognized that the therapist's personality, demeanor, and life experience interact in particular ways with each patient. Roy Schafer put it aptly, "As an analyst one empathizes with one's idea of the analysand" (1983, 39). Some aspects of the therapist's personality may evoke conflict and anxiety, while other aspects may merge comfortably and sometimes unnoticeably (Caligor 1980). Carrying this notion to its logical conclusion, Levenson (1972) notes that "each therapist will hear in the sequential exchange his own hermeneutics, his content," and this in turn means that some aspects of the patient will be better attended to than others.

The changes that become possible with a change of therapist are observed often in individual treatment. Trudy left treatment with her first therapist because of a complex interaction of relationship difficulties and transferential issues. Trudy was thirty when she went into analysis. Her mother, a war refugee, had been abandoned by her husband. Trudy never really knew her father. She grew up skilled at adapting to the needs of others. Repeated relationships with older men seemed to reflect the absence of a father in her formative years.

Trudy's first analyst was experienced, well-trained, and known for his particular interest in the traumatic effects of social upheavals on personality. In treatment, Trudy developed strong positive feelings for the analyst and was able to review her early years in the safety of his consistent, attentive responsiveness. Her pattern of always leaving relationships changed, and Trudy married. Her husband was a strong, authoritarian, older man very much in love with her. However, Trudy continued to be unable to express real differences with her analyst or with her husband, despite their active encouragement for her to do so. She remained in a father-daughter relationship with each of them.

Unable to get beyond this impasse over many months, Trudy went for consultation with another analyst, a woman. After a series of exploratory sessions and a great deal of turmoil, she decided to transfer. She found this analyst particularly attuned to her conflicts and the working alliance very different. As the new treatment progressed, Trudy began to move beyond her impasse. Her work with the first analyst had led to important changes but had precluded the possibility of others.

The limitations of particular dyads are often seen with patients who have previously been in therapy with competent therapists. They come to therapy the second time angry and disappointed at what didn't happen the first time.

Combined Therapy and Developmental Theory

The sequences of combined analytic treatments are analogous to, but not synonomous with, the developmental sequence of separation and individuation as described by Mahler, Pine, and Bergmann (1975). The effectiveness of therapy stems in part from the opportunity to reexperience the separation-individuation sequence with the therapist as the central person. Combined therapy extends this one step further, to the group with the therapist.

It is clear that one doesn't really start all over again in the therapeutic relationship. However, there seem to be curative possibilities in the fantasies of merging, being responded to, and understood and safe in the idealized transference to the omnipotent therapist, and then individuating.

The sequence described by Mahler (et al 1975) moves from normal autism to successful separation and individuation, object constancy and healthy self-esteem.

The analogy with normal developmental sequence can help us understand the sequence of combined therapy and the particularities of the transition of the patient from individual to combined therapy. Some patients appear to regress in their behavior and experience themselves as worse when they move from individual therapy to combined therapy. The pressure of the group's presence is experienced as a failure of therapist empathy. The patient feels deprived of the organizing effect of the therapeutic relationship. When patients need the therapeutic symbiosis as a defense against the dissolution of the self, the addition of the group must be postponed.

When the patient is sufficiently developed so that it is enough that the therapist functions as a frame of reference and a point of orientation in the group, then he or she is ready for combined therapy. The level of frustration is increased for patients entering group from individual treatment, and they need to be able to function with some independence for the transition to be productive therapeutically.

In the practicing period of normal growing up, the development of autonomous apparatuses (Mahler, et al 1975), the child's "belief in his own magic omnipotence is still to a consid-

25

erable extent derived from his sense of sharing in his mother's magic powers" (p. 186). We see parallels in the patient who begins to move out into new behaviors and risk new experiences with the safety and power of a belief in the relationship with the therapist. Because of the therapist's attention to other group members, this aspect of the patient's relationship is temporarily strained in the transition to the group, but is subsequently resumed. And sometimes recent gains are temporarily lost in the stress of entering a group.

Veronica was a timid woman who had made great strides in her individual treatment. She had been afraid of the outside world, but with individual therapy she had been able to make forays into areas previously laden with fear and anxiety. She went out dancing with friends, bicycled in the park on her own, and took vacation trips. When she entered the group, these new activities were interrupted. Old excuses for not going out began to reappear, and for the first few group sessions she came in wearing the dark glasses she had given up months before. The loss of the exclusive relationship with her therapist induced Veronica to regress to her previous helpless state. In helping Veronica get beyond this, the therapist's role was very important in interpreting the meanings of her behaviorial change in her individual sessions as well as in the group. The therapist reminded Veronica of earlier fears of not being able to function independently and encouraged her to talk about these in the group. In both contexts the therapist maintained an atmosphere supportive to her individuation. Thus, when a group member asked Veronica why she wore dark glasses to group sessions, she was able to verbalize her conflict between achieving further growth and her anger at relinquishing her passive-dependent tie to the therapist, as well as its resultant anxiety. Veronica didn't want to see or be seen and, as a symbolic statement of this, had put on dark glasses.

In individual sessions, we see an analogue to what the toddler encounters in the period of rapprochement. Reality challenges the toddler's omnipotence, self-esteem can be deflated, and there is more vulnerability to shame in the presence of peers. Dependence upon an object who is now perceived as powerful but separate confronts a toddler with relative helplessness. During the comparable phase in therapy, it is important that the therapist maintains some of the organizing function and support of the therapeutic relationship for the patient to successfully manage a way through this. (This will be discussed in detail in chapter 3, which focuses on the period of transition from individual to combined treatment.)

The "True Self" and Combined Therapy

One of the consequences of unsuccessful separation and individuation is the development of what Donald Winnicott (1965) calls the "false self." This concept refers to persons behaving in a way geared to others' expectations rather than their own needs. This is most likely to develop when the parents are unresponsive, intrusive, or narcissistic. The false self is quickly spotted in a cohesive, sensitized group, which reacts to it as phony and inauthentic and will not value such behaviors. When they first enter group, patients may feel bewildered that this new world rejects what their original caretakers had valued. In the individual session these patients can be helped to cope with the tremendous anxiety stirred up by new responses to old defensive patterns. Examining this bewilder-

ment in the collaborative atmosphere of the individual relationship permits the patient to feel less anxious and vulnerable
and more ready to understand and change.

An example of "false self" behavior is seen in the case of
Louise, an attractive young lawyer who entered the group and
immediately evoked critical responses. Louise appeared to the
group "to have an answer for everything." Attractive, well-
dressed, obviously professionally successful, she quickly responded to other group members' problems. She would start
with, "It seems to me the problem is————" and proceed to
"You ought to————." The therapist was able to observe what
Louise had often reported in individual therapy sessions, that
everyone considered her to be a strong personality but got
annoyed with her. The therapist also saw that Louise in no way
revealed to the group the needy, dependent feelings that had
been part of her lifelong experience. Louise presented to the
group, as she did in most situations, the false self, the problem
solver.

When, after three weeks, Joseph, a critical voice in the
group, finally said, "Why are you here if you have all the
answers?" Louise fell silent and looked lost. After a moment
she responded in a soft voice, "But that is the problem. I come
on so strong, and I don't feel that way. I need help, and I
wonder why people are so angry with me. It is happening here,
too." The response of the group, as voiced by Joseph, touched
directly on what had been the focus of the individual therapy.
Louise appeared invulnerable, but she secretly felt like a weak
and needy child.

The group was able to help Louise look at the effects of the
defensive position she had adopted and how it had prevented
her from gaining what she needed. In the weeks that followed,
she was able to share her history with the group. It had been

explored in her individual therapy and the origins of her false self had been clarified; however, in the context of the group experience her history was reconstructed from a new perspective. As the group came to understand Louise's defensive needs for the false self, they were able to be more sympathetic and begin to work with her to modify this characterological defense, separating out her real strengths from her defensive posturing.

Expansion of Therapeutic Possibilities

Reexamination of Freud's metapsychological formulations has led to a more selective acceptance of Freud's theories. Parts of the metapsychology, the more abstract levels of generalization, have been rejected while the clinical theory, based on clinical observation, has been maintained (Silverman 1976, 622). The change has permitted more relevant and individualized approaches to patients, free of the constraints of some of the earlier Freudian theories. Nevertheless, the same dilemmas persist on the level of clinical theory. Taking a particular therapeutic stance offers advantages but frequently includes constraints. Combining analytic treatments offers an expansion of the therapeutic possibilities to reduce the limitations of the constraints.

The degree to which the analyst should remain personally opaque or responsive has been frequently debated and revised ever since the early encouragement that the analyst reveal nothing and remain a "blank screen." The traditional view that the analyst's neutrality encouraged the unfolding of the transference neurosis and the expression of both sides of the patient's ambivalence resulted in some analysts maintaining a cold, distant demeanor. However, the contemporary focus on the therapeutic relationship as providing not only the context of therapy, but also one of its curative dimensions, has changed attitudes toward neutrality and raised important technical questions. To some extent, the analyst's interactions geared to improving and maintaining the working alliance tend to reduce the blatant distortions and regression evoked by more restrained, less collaborative therapists of the past. This lessened ambiguity in the relationship can lead to less, or more subtle, distortions of perception within the analytic situation; a more rational perception; and less access to important irrational material. The addition of the group and the transference reactions activated by other group members can provide additional opportunities to experience intense transference distortions within the treatment situation. This is particularly true of negative responses, which are so fruitful for insight and understanding.

Sharon's relationship with her therapist, discussed earlier in this chapter, provides an apt example. Over the years of productive therapy together, a familiarity and trust had been established; within this comparatively less ambiguous relationship, there was less projection from Sharon. The therapist was consistently and empathically attuned to Sharon; rage or frustration in response to narcissistic injury was seldom experienced in the session. However, other relationships outside of the therapy posed sorry contrasts. Sharon was hurt and insulted again and again. For Sharon, no one could maintain the level of attunement of the analytic session.

When Sharon entered the group, the therapist was able to observe the kind of experiences she had been reporting in her sessions. Mild, sarcastic comments from other group members were experienced as painful assaults. A lack of appreciation from the group of her hypersensitivity to criticism felt like such a rebuff that Sharon would be silent for an entire session in response. Gently and gradually, first in the individual sessions and later in group, the therapist was able to work more directly toward Sharon's acknowledgment of her own hypersensitivity and toward building her tolerance and understanding of the responses of others.

Corrective Emotional Experience

The issue of the advantages and limitations of the "corrective emotional experience" has been debated since its introduction by Franz Alexander. Essentially the entire psychoanalytic therapy is a corrective emotional experience—the therapist is able to provide understanding, attentiveness, and appreciation while maintaining analytic neutrality. This is a constellation of conditions that every neurotic was deprived of in the past in one way or another. However, some analysts attempted to take the corrective emotional experience further by experimenting with deliberately offering the patient the emotional experience he was deprived of while growing up. Best known of the experiments was Sandor Ferenczi's, in which he experimented with giving the contact and admiration that the patient craved (Ferenczi 1955). However, these procedures tend to constrain the possibilities of the analytic process. If the therapist departs significantly from the position of analytic neutrality in individual treatment, there is serious interference with the therapy. If the therapist offers the corrective emotional experience outside of therapeutic parameters, the patient may experience it as manipulative, and it will probably interfere with the range of transference reactions the patient needs.

Departure from neutrality also interferes with the patient's development of autonomy. This problem is permitted some resolution by the addition of group. When another group member makes a suggestion or gives advice, it can be truly helpful, and different from early experience in the family of origin without interfering with the neutrality and the efficacy of the therapist.

An illustration of this occurred in Ralph's treatment. Ralph grew up with a father he could never please, so he developed a tendency to give up trying. At one session, Ralph sadly told the group that he was dismissed from his job for being ineffectual, expressing no difference or anger with the decision, which as he described it, sounded arbitrary. Phil, visibly annoyed by Ralph's attitude, exhorted him to make a list of all his accomplishments on the job and to actively fight the dismissal decision. Phil gave Ralph direct advice, indicating just what he had done when he had found himself in a similar situation. Phil's statement, "You're worth more than you think; I know just from the things you've told us in here," was very different from what Ralph's father would have said and from the response Ralph usually evoked in others. Ralph acted on Phil's advice, and got reinstated. This opened for exploration Ralph's perpetual need to play out the role of a helpless victim. The therapist was able to focus empathically on this issue, having observed Ralph's anticipation of failure unless challenged.

Characterological Defenses

The treatment of characterological defenses is another dilemma addressed by combining analytic treatments. As the character neurotic's defenses are ego-syntonic—that is, they seem perfectly natural—he or she has little or no access to the conflict which gave rise to the defense. The analysis may then become stalemated. However, productive confrontation of character defenses in individual treatment is a sensitive issue exaggerated by involvement of the transference. Confrontation can endanger the feeling of safety and trust the patient has experienced in individual treatment. Confrontation by the therapist is likely to be experienced as non-empathic, intrusive, or assaultive. But when the patient encounters the confrontation from peers in the group, it is another opportunity to consider it, with the therapist maintaining an empathic position toward the hurt it may pose. Therefore group therapy, added to individual therapy, offers a variety of balances for confronting characterological defenses. If the therapist is more confronting, support is usually more available from the group, and if the activity originates in the group, the therapeutic relationship is available for binding the anxiety and integrating the awareness.

An example of how helpful the group is in confronting characterological defenses can be seen in the case of Gregory. In individual therapy, Gregory had tended to be accommodating, submissive, and unassertive. He had come into therapy troubled by his submissive role in marriage and by his feelings of sexual inadequacy. Since he was so accommodating, he could not understand why his wife was so angry with him. He felt that the same dynamic occurred in his work situation—he gave much and received little. In individual therapy, Gregory had come to recognize the parallels between his present responses to his wife and past responses to his quietly controlling mother. He could begin to acknowledge the anger he had felt growing up in an extremely repressive environment, and the fury he had felt towards his father, who had passively accepted his mother's dominant position in the household.

Though Gregory could recognize some of the parallels to his

mother and wife in his responses to his female therapist, he could not acknowledge any feeling of anger toward her. Though the therapist worked with him to identify these feelings, especially when they appeared symbolically in dreams, or subtly exposed in "jokes," there was some unconscious collusion by the therapist with Gregory's denial of his anger, so that this apparently cooperative patient did not become aware of the anger he emanated.

After two years of individual therapy, group was added to Gregory's treatment. In the group, Gregory took on the role of "helper," telling people what they really felt and what they should do. Both Gregory and the therapist were able to observe his authoritarian behavior and his competitive feelings toward the therapist. Group members commented on these alternative behaviors. At first Gregory could not understand why his words, his attitude, indeed his very tone of voice evoked such anger in the group.

As Gregory's anger was worked on in the group and in individual therapy, Gregory finally voiced his feeling that he could not be angry with the therapist since she had been so generous with him. At the beginning of individual therapy an accommodation in fee had been made for Gregory, who earned very little in his job at a non-profit agency. In the group, he paid the same fee as the other patients. The conscious and unconscious meaning of this accommodation on the part of the therapist had to be worked through by Gregory. The therapist had to consider what her own unconscious motives may have been in making this special arrangement with the patient. Was it partly her way of seeking to identify with, or get approval from a man who was expending his considerable talents in public service work for very meager monetary rewards? For the therapist there is always a dramatic difference between hearing about and actually experiencing an aspect of the patient that is not readily revealed in the dyadic relationship. In this case, Gregory had told his therapist about his expression of anger, but she had never actually seen it played out as she did in the group setting. When the therapist experiences a sense of surprise, it usually signals countertransference feelings that have obscured the awareness of some aspect of the dyadic relationship. It was the therapist's countertransference to Gregory's particularly ego-syntonic defenses that had blocked development of this in individual treatment. In group, the confrontation of both situations unblocked aspects of the therapy and permitted it to develop freely.

The Inequality of the Analytic Relationship

The traditional non-egalitarian structure of the patient-therapist relationship in analysis poses yet another dilemma that can be helped by combined analytic therapies. The therapist is the knowing authority; the patient is the novice. While this structure may increase therapeutic effectiveness, it is not consistent with more adult functioning. Current psychoanalytic writings have elaborated on this. Erik Erikson has spelled out the crucial developmental tasks that are completed in the stages of development beyond childhood (1950). Margaret Mahler's formulations of separation and individuation as an ongoing process throughout the life of the individual has given us an appreciation of development in later phases (1975). In addition, existential and humanistic thinking in psychoanalysis in general has contributed to our awareness of the importance of equally respectful relationships.

Many therapists personally endorse egalitarian relationships and so are uncomfortable with the omniscience and superiority inevitably attributed to them. However, this inequality is part of the evolution of the analytic process and to deny it would introduce a distortion. This poses a unique problem in psychoanalytic treatment. Initially, the intrinsic inequality of the analytic relationship and the fantasies it promotes make analytic treatment possible. The fantasy of new strength in the relationship with the all-powerful analyst facilitates change. However, this same structure tends to tug against the developmental tasks of the later stages of treatment. In the working-through process, the development of a more autonomous, independent functioning and the ability to express and maintain differences with the analyst are most important.

The gradual resolution of the transference reduces the fantasy distortions of the analyst as all-powerful, but the experience the patient has had in the relationship up until then persists and is difficult to modify. Entry into the group helps at this stage. It promotes further resolution of transference distortions. The actual situation of being in a group with other people and the analyst challenges both the transferential and the reality aspects of the analytic relationship.

The transference aspects become more apparent as the group members hear that the same therapist is experienced as both warm and cold, intimidating and unthreatening, authoritarian and permissive. The very nature of transference becomes more comprehensible as patients observe others repeating patterns they evidence with the analyst with other group members; for example, the man who reacts to one woman after another as castrating, or the woman who repeatedly views others as insufficiently appreciative or attentive.

In addition, as a group member the patient experiences a

more powerful and autonomous role. Among peers, accustomed dependency on the therapist is modified as the patient experiences helping others. The therapy relationship becomes less uneven and more balanced.

A model of therapy that combines individual and group work leaves us with the vast number of ambiguities psychotherapy poses, but it does increase our options. It is not offered as a solution for all the problems of therapy or for all patients. The following chapter will consider some of the variations and diagnostic considerations that are important in making the choice of combined analytic therapy.

CHAPTER 2

The Analytic Group: Considerations in Recommending It for the Individual Patient

THE DECISION to add group therapy to the treatment is based on the therapist's diagnostic understanding of the patient's treatment as it has progressed, the patient's own goals, and motivation to pursue these. The analyst who decides to do this includes in his or her evaluation of the patient the consideration that group evokes unique reactions from individuals, responses that might not ever be in evidence in other interactions. Adding group to the treatment significantly expands the context of therapy, but it is important to gauge the patient's readiness for it.

Both social psychologists and therapists who have worked with small groups have observed that, for most people, entry into a group creates anxiety. A number of explanations have been offered for this. Freud saw the regression of the individual in the group as universal. His observation, based on the work of the social psychologist William McDougall (1920), saw individuals relinquishing some of their competence and aggression to maintain their safety in the group. The price the individual pays is increased dependency and its concomitant anxiety. For Freud, this was related to oedipal issues—the fear of the primal father, and the capitulation to him.

Wilfred Bion (1961), influenced by Kleinian thinking, saw the group as inducing even more primitive regressive experiences. His notion of the regression induced by the group suggests that the initial anxiety resonates with archaic experiences like the infant's early experience at the mother's breast. In Bion's view, "splitting" (a tendency to experience people as all good or all bad); "projective identification" (experiencing denied attributes of the self in others); and idealization are more likely to take place in the group.

Related to Bion's formulations is Otto Kernberg's more recent observation that groups activate archaic internalized objects. Even in highly trained, relatively healthy, mature professionals, this was observed. Conducting training groups, Kernberg found that there was a remarkable activation of primitive emotional processes in these unstructured group situations (Kernberg 1976, 250).

Experimental studies in laboratory conditions by social psychologists have demonstrated that the mere presence of others while doing a task can increase tension (Zajonc and Sales 1966). This additional tension can either promote or diminish task effectiveness, depending upon the nature of the task and the individual's prior knowledge and competence.

The therapist juxtaposes an understanding of these general

reactions to group with an understanding of the individual patient when making the decision to add group to the treatment. The extended nature of individual treatment permits the therapist to estimate the amount of disorganization or regression that entry into the group would be likely to precipitate for the patient, and the point at which the patient is ready to cope with it.

Timing of the Entry into Group

The therapist considers adding group when he or she feels that aspects of the therapy best dealt with in individual therapy have been accomplished; when there is a collaborative understanding of history as related to current functioning; when there is an awareness of the quality of the transference; and when there is a solid, working alliance. This means that the patient and the therapist have worked and struggled together, and that the patient has been able to tolerate the differences between them and learn from the experience without regressing for more than a temporary or brief period.

Combined analytic treatment requires that the patient has sufficient ego strength and a level of social development that provide the abilities to understand the needs of others separate from the self, with the implicit recognition that others have independent volition. That is, a patient must be able to tolerate another person's concern with what may seem trivial, like someone being upset over not receiving a phone call from a new friend while the patient is coping with serious illness in the family and urgently needs support and understanding.

To be ready for group entry, there must also be a capacity to work with transference reactions displaced onto group members and to process feedback about oneself. For example, George felt a burst of impatience towards a group member triggered by the "silly" movement of her hand, reminiscent of his mother. George could see that his destructive outburst was exaggerated and stemmed from early frustrations with his mother's "silliness," which always got in the way. These capacities to work with transference reactions will develop and grow in treatment, but will fluctuate during the process.

The criteria for combined therapy leave room for a wide variety of patients. Most patients who can use analytic therapy could benefit from the addition of group, but practical considerations of time, confidentiality, and sometimes finances, frequently preclude it or make it not worth it. It is necessary for patients to be aware of their needs for merging and dependency to tolerate separateness and difference with the therapist in the group. A measure of this is the patient's capacity to accept the therapist's empathy for transferential wishes rather than to expect actual gratification within the transference. The therapist may empathize with the wish for a personal, parental response and yet not provide it. This does not take away the patient's need for symbiotic relatedness, but means the patient becomes more aware of it and is better able to modulate it.

Patients will differ on how long they spend in individual therapy before the optimal point for the addition of group. Less integrated patients, with more pathology, need a longer time in the individual treatment phase. Severely narcissistic patients may need an extended period of individual treatment before they can tolerate the shifting focus of attention in a group (an example was Susan in chapter 1). These patients need careful preparation in individual treatment prior to entry into group, gradually learning to tolerate empathic failures without massive disorganization.

In response to the therapist's suggestion of adding group, the patient may feel pushed, abandoned, or exploited with thoughts like, "You're tired of me boring you," or "You probably need a kook like me in your group," or "How come you're taking a position of recommending something instead of analyzing it?"

The rationale for answering the latter question is that the recommendation for group *is* a treatment decision offered as a recommendation to the patient, like the number of individual sessions a week. The patient will, or will not, choose to go along with it.

The quality of the transference is an important indicator for planning combined analytic treatment and differentiating between narcissistic and neurotic patients. Both forms of transference are impinged upon with entry into group, but it is more likely that the neurotic patient will work through entry more productively. When transferences are essentially neurotic, the analysis of the resistance to entering group is usually quite productive. Central issues in the patient's original family tend to underlie much of the resistance to entering group—the fear of not getting attention when other members are present, the fear of abandonment, or hypersensitivity to being controlled or exploited.

For neurotic patients, transferences tend to surface with more clarity and become more accessible as group is added to individual therapy. Subtle dependencies and accommodations to the therapist, suppressed resentments, and a variety of distortions become heightened. The patient may feel controlled, tricked, or otherwise manipulated as he experiences the anxiety over entry into the group. The patient's ability to work analytically and to process all of this can make entry into group a most productive phase of treatment.

Introducing group to patients with more narcissistic attributes can result in excessive fragmentation and loss of cohesion. The resulting demands on the group, as well as on the patient, are not productive for therapy. It is not always possible to predict accurately the amount of disorganization the group will induce in the narcissitic patient, or whether the disruption will be ultimately therapeutic, but the following examples of a more neurotic and a more narcissistic type of patient will be of some help to the reader.

Like many accommodating neurotic patients, Lloyd's behavior upon entry to group was quite different from the open, spontaneous, and confident manner he evidenced in individual treatment. In relation to group members, he became more anxious, tense, and oppositional. These aspects of Lloyd had existed in his individual sessions, but to such a mild and slight degree that they were often subliminal for the therapist. Lloyd's intense competitive feelings emerged in the group when he had to compete with peers and share his therapist.

Analysis of the difference in the two settings produced awareness of the quality of Lloyd's exclusive relationship to the therapist and, implicit in this, the repetition of his particular oedipal resolutions. In Lloyd's father's absence, Lloyd got along too well with his mother. With both parents present he had tended to get more anxious and to regress to "silly," demanding, or provocative behavior.

Similarly, in group Lloyd would frequently get silly and demand excessive attention. This would evoke irritation, avoidance, and rejection from the group. Subsequent individual sessions provided the opportunity to link this behavior to history and to Lloyd's anxiety in situations where he had to compete with others or work collaboratively.

Possessing the ego strengths and the quality of a resilient working alliance necessary, Lloyd's entry to group at this point was most productive for treatment. Continued analysis of his contrasting reactions in both settings helped to clarify and elucidate the total nature of his essentially neurotic transference reaction.

Natalie, more narcissistic and less individuated, did not make the transition to group successfully. She was so bewildered at the group's confrontation about characterological problems she was only beginning to be aware of and change, that she became confused and overwhelmed. She was not ready to give up the merging quality of her narcissistic transference with her therapist during the time that she was in the group. The discontinuity of her therapist in individual sessions and group was intolerable to Natalie. After a few weeks, it was agreed, at least for the present, that she should withdraw from the group.

A Note on Narcissism

An understanding of our view of narcissism is central to understanding the discussion of planning combined analytic therapy. In general, our clinical observations regarding the narcissistic aspects of patients are best explained by the formulations of Kohut (1977), Gedo (1979, 1981), and Stolorow and Lachman (1980). Narcissism is seen as a product of certain developmental traumas resulting in fixed characterological responses. These writers on narcissism have separated the observational data of traditional psychoanalysis from the libido theory to which it was originally connected. Thus, the existence of narcissistic behavior in adult life is understood as indicating pathological vulnerability in the sphere of self-esteem rather than excessive self-love. Patients who are self-preoccupied, unable to be concerned with others, who lack the ability to respond empathically, and who may be exhibitionistic in their behavior are understood as demonstrating pathological vulnerability in adult life resulting from early injuries to basic self-esteem. Relationships are viewed as providing a substitute for the missing or defective self-esteem and are unconsciously structured in terms of how they can best serve to maintain and sustain a cohesive sense of self (Stolorow and Lachman 1980, 113).

When we speak of narcissistic behavior and the narcissistic patient, and neurotic behavior or the neurotic patient, we are not talking about discrete categories but rather the predominant mode. Clinical observations are considered as occurring on a continuum. Each person fluctuates among different levels of integration and functioning, so that Susan (chapter 1) in her individual session, was responsive, relaxed, and gratified. In group she became glazed, unrelated, and terribly anxious in a manner that was not observable in the individual session. For the therapist's response to be most empathic, it must be in terms of the level of integration represented by the behavior (Gedo 1979, 1981). Thus in individual sessions the therapist could offer verbal interpretations that were heard and accepted. In group, Susan needed the therapist to pick up, through eye contact, that she felt immobilized, anxious, and needed to have the therapist articulate this for her during the group session.

In planning combined therapy, it is important for the therapist to understand the particular meaning of the narcissistic responses of the patient, but it is also important for patients to have some understanding of their own behavior, identifying its origins in terms of their own histories.

To participate in group therapy, an important ability is willingness and readiness to at times view others as separate from one's own needs. In order to function in a group, the patient has to have reached the point where he or she will be able to maintain integration when faced with empathic failure from one or another of the group members. Natalie could not tolerate the group's lack of understanding or acceptance of her unarticulated preoccupation with her pressing need for bolstering and attention, so she became increasingly disorganized in group. Since it began to affect every aspect of her life, the addition of group was not a productive therapeutic move.

The strength of the working alliance with the therapist and the resilience of the alliance determines why some patients can tolerate the fluctuations they experience in group while others can not. Back in the safety of the dyad, the patient can usually make progress towards understanding a catastrophic reaction experienced in group. The therapist can use observations from the group session in the safety of the individual session, so that the patient experiences the therapist as more empathic. However, for some patients, this is not always sufficient. Slight paranoid propensities in a patient, for example, can balloon in a group situation and disrupt the patient-therapist relationship, seriously impeding progress for the total therapy.

Addressing the Symbiotic Aspects of the Therapeutic Relationship

The crucial issue at the point of adding group to the therapy is that the patient-therapist interaction has included conflict and struggle. This means that there has been sufficient disruption of the symbiotic transference for the patient to reexperience the traumatic effects of childhood disillusionments with the idealized parental object (Gedo 1981, 117). This process of "optimal disillusionment" is most effectively dealt with first in the individual phase of combined therapy. In cases where extensive hostility or rejection were actually leveled at the patient in childhood, there is frequently a need to hold on tenaciously to an idealized picture of the therapy and of the therapist.

After a year and a half of individual analytic treatment Amy (discussed in chapter 1 and later in this chapter) would still go into depressive slumps when confronted with the reality that the therapist could not always know what she felt when she did not articulate it, and could not transform her, only help her to grow and help herself. It was crucial for Amy to experience this and work with it in the exclusively individual phase of treatment to prepare her for the more autonomous functioning that would be required of her in group.

Considerations for the Therapist in Adding Group

The composition of the patient's family should be taken into consideration when placing him in a group. For example, patients who grew up as only children have a particularly difficult time adjusting to group. Nevertheless, however hard the transition is for them, the difficulties have been demonstrated to be worth it.

Helen, a socially outgoing twenty-six-year-old, was the adored only child of a career woman. She was showered with the love and attention her mother could not give to either her first husband, Helen's father, or her second husband, who was an attentive stepparent. Helen came to treatment because of difficulty she was having in a current relationship with a man despite the fact that she was attractive, sexually responsive, and men were initially drawn to her.

Helen's strengths made her a good analytic patient. She was intelligent, open, and perceptive; she worked productively in three sessions a week. After a year-and-a-half, the therapist had not suggested group. Helen was working through some fairly severe narcissistic issues with reasonably sustained productive effort. Group might have intruded upon this experience, resulting in a premature closing up and defensiveness. In the transference, Helen was struggling with individuation from the therapeutic symbiosis, in which she was reexperiencing the intense ambivalence of her relationship with mother.

At this point in individual treatment, Helen began to ask about going into a group. She had seen group members laughing and joking in a waiting room before her session, and wanted to have that apparent sense of belonging. Her conscious fantasy, which she related in her session, was to be the charming center of the therapist's group. The therapist thought Helen was partly seeking some replenishment for the narcissistic gratification that she had been losing in individual treatment as she was confronted with some of her characterological defenses.

The therapist weighed the considerations for Helen joining group. On the negative side was the possibility of Helen's prematurely distancing from involvement in the individual sessions as she moved to group, resulting from the defensive behavior she would need there. But this negative was outweighed by the positive side, which was the strong working alliance, the substantial ego strength, and Helen's healthy wish to be more separate and independent. The fact that Helen was an only child predicted an extended time in group in order for it to constitute a truly corrective experience. But there was a readiness in Helen's attitude for intimate experience with peers which she had missed. Helen's lack of this experience tended to perpetuate itself in current social distancing with others.

As had been anticipated, the first six months in group were extremely difficult for Helen. The extent to which she antagonized the other patients surprised the therapist and gave some indication that there was more countertransference operative than had been realized. Helen's rather arrogant, self-indulgent manner and limited awareness of her impact on other's sensitivities evoked a good deal of resentment from the group, emerging in the form of criticisms and put-downs. The reaction Helen evoked was exaggerated and rationalized by her comparatively fortunate circumstances financially, socially, and intellectually. Some group members envied her complete lack of concern about money; others her access to interesting and prominent people; and still others her advanced education. Their envy blocked empathy for Helen's vulnerability. It was difficult for people to feel concern for the sensibilities of someone who seemed objectively more fortunate.

Helen was devastated by the negative reaction she experienced in the group. She had had little experience with direct and open rejection and criticism in the carefully programmed life she had led. The therapist made comments in the group to convey her empathy with Helen's hurt and dismay, as well as with other members' defensive reactions toward Helen. Intervening at this point was helpful for the evolving group process. Permitting more acting out of the interaction was judged not to be constructive for both the group and Helen.

It was months before Helen could comprehend what it was about her that was offending people so, but gradually she was able to understand and break through the narcissistic encasement that had kept her isolated and lonely. The feedback Helen received from group members spelled out the resentment and envy she evoked.

The complex interaction of Helen's provocation and the group members' envy and resentment had to be unraveled for each individual. Sometimes it happened in group. For example, the therapist said to a man who was having financial difficulties supporting his family, "It must be hard to tolerate Helen's lack of concern about money when it's such a painful scarcity for you." In an individual session a woman from a very deprived socioeconomic background confessed that she felt envious of the family Helen had and the opportunities it offered. She was impatient with Helen's lack of appreciation for it, and would have loved to change places.

Helen's working alliance with the therapist deepened as she brought to her individual sessions the hurt she had felt in group. Despite the stress and the anxiety stirred up by the group, she was able to work productively in her individual sessions on what was happening in it, what was happening in her fantasies and experiences with the therapist, and what was happening elsewhere in her life.

Request for Group as an Acting Out in the Transference

Sometimes a patient directly expresses a wish to enter a group, and it is interpreted by the therapist as something that would interfere with rather than promote the treatment process. The desire to enter a group may be an expression of resistance to individual therapy.

Annette's case is an example of transference resistance. A rather brittle young woman, she was involved in an intense libidinized transference to her male analyst and was continually pressing to join his group. Unable to tolerate the anxiety required to deal with her intense oedipal conflicts, Annette's wish was to act out by removing herself from the intimacy of the relationship with her therapist. Exploration of her motivation revealed that the wish to go into group was primarily regressive and defensive in nature. In the transference, Annette was reexperiencing the difficulty of separating from an infantile mother, which had been complicated by her father's alternation of absence and aggression. Although she was aware of her rage toward her mother, there had been no father to move toward. Until these painful issues were worked with and identified, entry into group would have been more a product of collusion with acting out than a significant developmental step in analysis. The therapist believed that Annette was marginally capable of functioning in group in terms of ego strength, but the contraindication for adding group at this time was that she would have been avoiding dealing with a crucial step in the analytic process.

With each patient, what determines timing is the relative merit between what is gained and what is lost by entering into combined therapy at a certain point. With Annette, delaying entry into group until she could better understand her transference reactions, including her wish to escape into group, helped clarify the therapeutic process even though it prolonged total treatment. For Helen, entering group when she did created more time for gaining important missed experiences that she needed to integrate after getting beyond the fairly set characterological defenses she was accustomed to using to ward off intimacy in her relationships. However, there was a possibility that there would be some short circuiting in working out some of the transferences.

Individual History

In planning for group, a patient's peer group experience and recent history is crucial. A person who has always felt like an outsider in groups, or who has had difficulty in a particular group setting usually needs an extended individual phase of therapy to cope with the terror that coming into group may represent.

An extreme situation that illustrates the need for extended individual therapy is Amy, the single woman in her thirties discussed in chapter 1, who came for consultation in an anxious, agitated state. Amy had been in combined treatment for five years and had found the individual sessions extremely frustrating and the group sessions devastating. She had experienced her former analyst as cold, impersonal, and distant in the individual session, and had felt betrayed by him when he did not intervene when she felt attacked in the group.

Amy's rigid character structure, her proclivity toward becoming immobilized and panicked with anxiety, her terror of new situations, and a tendency to retreat to masochistic defenses had placed her in a treatment impasse. The worse Amy felt, the less able she was to move out of her treatment situation. A chance encounter and conversation with a woman who had left the group encouraged Amy to follow her lead and go for a consultation. After a series of consultations, Amy left combined treatment and started in individual treatment with the new therapist, for whom she had formed an immediate attachment. The therapist did not recommend group, and this had Amy's wholehearted approval.

After two-and-one-half years of sessions twice a week, the therapist considered group for Amy. Amy's history of feeling inadequate and peripheral in peer groups; a paucity of peer group experience; an extremely compliant, dependent attachment to her new therapist; and a life history of being overprotected all indicated that group could make a substantial contribution to treatment. Although these factors also explained how group had been so devastating in Amy's previous treatment, she now had some of the strengths required for it. She was able to form relationships and had a capacity for self-awareness that had become more pronounced in treatment. Amy and her therapist had gradually drawn a more lucid picture of the connection between her present difficulties and her childhood as a sensitive, awkward child whose solution for coping was to withdraw, deny, avoid, and fantasize.

However, the negative experience that Amy had already had with group therapy required extra caution before more group treatment was undertaken. She was encouraged to review the experience she had had in the first group where, "They told me all the things I've always dreaded were true, such as I'm a hopeless case, hostile, frigid, and unattractive." The therapist empathized with how dreadful it must have felt. She encouraged Amy to review other peer experiences and the real and imagined hurts in those. It was only after an extended period of focusing on these aspects in individual treatment that the therapist felt able to risk recommending group. Amy gave the reaction that the therapist had anticipated: "You tell me to; I will. But I'm terrified. I want to believe that it can be different, but it's hard to imagine." The therapist noted Amy's usual masochistic response and held to the recommendation. She had learned from much experience with Amy that analytic neutrality required not getting caught up in Amy's exaggerated fears of new situations, which took the form of a communication that the action of the therapist was wounding her.

Amy's anxiety was excruciating in her initial group, but she was able to handle it with limited bursts of masochistic, self-defeating behaviors. The working alliance was strong and held up in her individual sessions and in her group. Within a year, Amy had the positive experience of becoming an active and effective member of a well-functioning group with which she valued affiliation, and of becoming significantly more autonomous and assertive in relation to her therapist.

Composition of the Analytic Group

The analytic groups we have been discussing are ongoing groups. That is, individual patients enter and terminate according to their own treatment needs, perhaps staying in a group for as long as three or four years. These patients all will have accomplished the tasks in individual treatment required for entry into group. The group's size may vary from six to nine, a range that seems to work well clinically—perhaps because this number is large enough to feel like a group and yet small enough to permit real intimacy.

Group members usually represent a range of ages, marital and socioeconomic statuses, and professions. An important consideration is for the patient to be sufficiently similar to other group members to feel comfortable. Research from a number of areas indicates that a person who is significantly different from all other members on any dimension is less likely to obtain benefits from group therapy (Yalom 1975, 227; Lieberman, Yalom and Miles 1973). This results from difficulties in empathizing due to envy of differences, discomfort with them, or simply lack of experience with them; one older person in a group of young adults, one black person in an all-white group, one poor person in a group of wealthy members are all undesirable situations. On the other hand, a diversity of dynamics and character structures among group members is desirable and vitalizes the group. It is preferable to combine impulsive people with over-restrained ones, intellectual types with more intuitive types, and so forth.

A narrow range of ego strength and degree of vulnerability in the patient's balance is recommended. People who are well defended and resilient can cope with all kinds of confrontation and challenge, though they might not welcome it. Those who are less well defended may be undermined by aggressive confrontation and require a more supportive group. A person should be in a group that is as confrontational and free to deal with reality as the patient is capable of coping with. Each group develops characteristics and norms of its own, and these should be considered before placing the patient in it.

Relationship with the Therapist

The working alliance the patient establishes with the therapist in individual treatment extends into the group. There is an agreement and a trust that the collaborative effort will continue, that group is meant to amplify individual therapy, and that working with other group members will be part of this amplification. Patients will show transference reactions they have had to the therapist in individual therapy to other group members.

Non-transferential relationships to other group members are clearly different from those established with the therapist. In a group, the patient is encouraged to respond with feelings and reactions, rational or irrational. Acting like a therapist characterizes an intellectualized, interpretive approach to other group members. This is a caricature of the therapist and is seen as resistance.

Members of a group are encouraged to react with feeling responses to another person's narrative or behavior. For example, a divorced man tells of his child's phone call from another state, where the child is living with his mother. The child reports being mistreated. Open, feeling responses from other group members are: "I can feel with him, so abandoned, so helpless," and "How guilty you must feel. That's why I stay in my marriage. I couldn't deal with it," and "You tell this so calmly. I can't stand it." In contrast, resistance responses are characterized by: "How did you feel when he said that?" and "Clearly you need to think through some plans," reflecting that these group members are distancing themselves emotionally, using thoughts instead of feelings in response to the original speaker.

The working alliance with the therapist essentially remains constant, its context extended as the patient enters the group. Entry into group may strain the working alliance because of the patient's heightened anxiety, but it doesn't really change its character.

Group Rules

In general, the parameters of the individual session are extended into the group with special consideration for the new form of therapy. Each group has its own rules and regulations, explicitly spelled out prior to becoming a member. Time, fees, the expectation that people attend regularly are all discussed by the therapist in the individual session.

An important new issue is confidentiality. In individual therapy, it is between the patient and therapist. In the group, others are involved. It is essential that confidentiality be understood and agreed upon by all members. Communications in the group should remain among group members and not be revealed to friends or family. It is a necessary condition for the open atmosphere of the group. The therapist intervenes when members reveal breaking confidentiality without awareness, saying, for example, "I told my wife," referring to some group material. If no other group member intervenes after a moment or two, the therapist, reinforcing the group rules, takes this responsibility.

The assumption is that understandings and information from individual sessions will be brought into the group by the patient. An initial lag before bringing new information into the group is generally understood. Patients need to feel less vulnerable and more familiar with new insights before they are comfortable sharing with the group. Prolonged holding back in the group is seen as resistance and analyzed as such, usually first in the individual session. On occasion, the therapist may want to initiate introducing information or a dynamic formulation arrived at in the individual session. We recommend checking this with the patient, either in the individual session or right in the group session, so that the patient feels essentially in charge of the manner and the rate at which revelations are made to fellow group members.

Members are expected to limit their interactions with each other to the group sessions. It permits more freedom of expression in the group when it is known that therapeutic interaction will not extend into the outside world of the patient. The patient is freer to express negative feelings and thoughts, real and transferential. In this way, the therapeutic context is protected from impingements that would dilute it. Nevertheless, exchanges that do occur outside are expected to be brought into the session for all to share so they can be understood in terms of the meaning to the participants and in terms of acting out behavior.

The general analytic rule for group is to stay aware of one's emotional responses to others' communications and behaviors, and to share as much of this awareness as possible.

Subgroupings and Alliances in Group

Within any group, individuals with reciprocal character traits always find each other. The therapist tries to maintain some kind of balance in the types of defensive structures of the patients in the group and therefore makes it even more likely that natural pairings emerge. You can count on the sadist always finding the masochist and the two engaging again and again. In one group, somebody who had been badly treated as a child instinctively sensed another person in the group who was a child beater. They engaged in many encounters before their reciprocal histories emerged. The seducer in the group always finds that person who is always feeling seduced, and the person who needs to control always finds somebody who will accommodate.

Mary, whose tendency was to project her frailties onto another person whom she would then proceed to take care of, found Edgar. He was someone who would take care of himself by accommodating to an admired caretaker. Edgar consistently responded to Mary's questions about how he felt or how he was doing. Mary would start group after group with this query. Eventually, Edgar began to resent her queries as intrusive and tried to understand what his participation with her meant. This became important material to be discussed in the group both for him and Mary. In individual sessions the therapist helped Mary to realize that she used projective identification as both a defense and an indirect communication to Edgar about what she really wanted (care and loving). Working in his individual treatment, Edgar began to see his transferential needs to accommodate Mary and experienced his resentment at being controlled by the role she was projecting onto him and that he was unconsciously accepting.

In another group, a man who was consistently passive-aggressive became very involved with an overtly aggressive member of the group. Each time the latter began to speak, the passive one subtly encouraged him to get angrier and more aggressive with other group members. At one point the therapist, to address the dynamics of the interaction, said, "This sounds like, 'Let's fight; I'll hold your coat.' " Both men were ready for the intervention. Each showed a glint of recognition and relaxed a bit as the group laughed.

Other subgrouping categories occur spontaneously in group, and as they occur are examined and understood. Groups may divide themselves along sex lines or in terms of marital status. In some groups, subgroupings evolve around the differences between achievers and non-achievers or between the affluent and those who are struggling economically. In another group, the division was expressed in terms of the group members who were therapists and those who were the "civilians." Noting and understanding the dynamics of these subgroupings provide valuable data for the individual and for the group.

Language and Mythology

Each group develops its own language, words having particular associated meanings rooted in shared history or shared emotional responses which many members identify with at different times. Each group also develops a mythology that arises out of its shared history and usually centers around a person who evokes strong affects, impulses, or characteristics which are meaningful for the group.

Abby was a particularly effective, articulate woman. She held strong opinions and expressed them with great style and had come to represent an admired ideal. She was the person both the men and the women of the group said they would like to emulate. She was the admired older sister. The group was also aware of how she used her extraordinary verbal ability to ward off intimacy and defend against strong feelings. As the defensive nature of her behavior changed, the real verbal skill remained, and "being like Abby" became a model of how to be expressive and articulate. Group members regarded her as a standard even after she left the group.

Marla represents another instance of group myth. She was so nervous at her first session that she literally fell out of her chair. As new members entered the group, she reassured them that they, too, would be confident as she now appeared to be by relating the incident of her first session. Thus, "like Marla" became the group's story to express anxiety on entering a group and sympathy for the tensions of the new member.

When John entered the group, he was a symbol of insensitivity. He came into the group taking no time to look around to see who was in the room with him, announced himself as a "captain of industry," addressed the women of the group as

"Honey," and attempted to take over as "chairman of the board." In time he began to recognize some of his objectionable behavior as defensive, and eventually he modified it. When it would reappear, people would remind him that he sounded like "that other John." "That other John" took its place in the group's mythology as the image for self-centered and unrelated behavior in a group.

The Case of Kenneth

The case of Kenneth gives us an opportunity to examine in detail the total treatment of a patient when considering combined treatment therapy for him.

Kenneth, a fifty-two-year-old engineer, came to treatment as a result of difficulties he could no longer ignore in his second marriage. The precipitating crisis was an affair his wife had engaged in after he had completely disregarded her attempts to communicate with him. Kenneth had been in therapy briefly twice before, unsuccessfully. He now felt he ought to look into himself before he lost the woman he really cared for.

During the initial consultation, the therapist encountered an intellectualized man who had little understanding of his impact on others. The quality of Kenneth's relationships was illustrated by his statement, "My worst impulse buying has to do with residences, used cars, and women." He described sex with his wife as "poking around." However, he also showed an interest in learning about himself and accepted the idea that he was at least partly responsible for his marital difficulties. He accepted intellectually that there could be some relationship between his current difficulties and his life story, and it was on this basis that treatment proceeded.

Initially, Kenneth preferred to sit up for his sessions rather than use the couch as the therapist suggested. After some time, however, he agreed to use the couch in twice-a-week analytic therapy. Though guarded, Kenneth seemed to enjoy the analytic experience and the opportunity to speak about himself. As he went on, his wit and humor began to emerge in occasional quips to the therapist. Kenneth had lived a life of relative isolation and had had little inclination or opportunity to share his inner thoughts and feelings. An only child of divorced parents who eventually remarried each other, he had lived with his father during his latency years and felt abandoned by his mother. Kenneth's physical needs had been functionally met, but there had been little warmth in his family life.

Kenneth was pleasantly surprised that the therapist was actually interested in his inner thoughts and feelings. He felt that neither parent had shown much empathy for his needs as a child, nor had they taken an interest in listening to him while he was growing up. Kenneth described his mother as a wet blanket and his father as a left-wing dissident given to violent rages until he was "blue in the face." His father would lecture him on politics or science, and Kenneth recalled his attempt to teach him Russian by speaking only that language and refusing to speak English for a month. Kenneth recalled, "It drove me up the wall, but I didn't say anything."

A beginning sense of a working alliance was established through the initial dreams Kenneth had in treatment. In the receptive setting of the therapy relationship, which he experienced as a special opportunity, Kenneth had begun to recall his dreams. His first dream was about "a group of Indians who were dancing." He didn't know if it was a war dance or a harvest celebration, but it was stimulating. "Some of the Indians ate some crows. Other crows were sitting around expectantly, and when the Indians danced, they danced, too." A second dream involved "a group of Arabs streaming and running through a ten-mile northern corridor of Israel." Kenneth recalled feeling frightened and puzzled by both dreams.

Surprised that he could produce such intriguing images, Kenneth was motivated to understand his internal world, which was so different from his view of himself as intellectual and logical, a view that he had tried to maintain and that he consciously valued. In his associations to these dreams, he recognized how much he felt passive and frightened and how much more he identified with these aspects of himself rather than with his aggressive aspects. The group of Indians dancing and his fear of them seemed to represent Kenneth's terror of his impulsive feelings and how much he tried to distance these from himself and projected them onto the environment. The crow paralleled two aspects of himself: an image of himself as black and ugly, and his fear of women, whom he experienced as devouring, capable of swallowing him up.

As therapy progressed, Kenneth came to understand that the Arab and Indian images were connected with his anxiety about expressing untamed feelings. He experienced these feelings as alien and primitive and therefore projected them in the dream as foreign figures. Kenneth sought to disavow these untamed feelings in his everyday life by objectifying some relationships and withdrawing from others.

The initial dream work helped Kenneth to see the connections between his inner experiences and outer behavior, and moved him toward reflecting on how experiences in his early life had shaped his present-day character. Kenneth moved into a compliant therapeutic relationship in which he idealized the therapist as a caring mother who would not abandon him prematurely, a mother whose judgment was sound, not a wet blanket who would stifle his creative interests. The therapist was a person who, in contrast to his father, could understand his language and who would not arbitrarily require him to speak another tongue.

The only expression of negative feelings toward treatment was when Kenneth would say that the requirements of therapy were occasionally inconvenient, with its demands on time or money. But then Kenneth would counter his own complaints by saying, "Actually it's not that bad."

A turning point in treatment came when Kenneth brought in a scientific paper he had written for the therapist to read. The therapist's response was to empathize with Kenneth's need for recognition from him, but then went on to ask for Kenneth's associations to the meaning of his request rather than reading the paper. Kenneth felt keen disappointment in not getting the gratification of the therapist's response to his paper. He reexperienced his frustrations with his father. He had often wished he had some father other than his own. "I was unhappy with him as my father, though I loved him. In his own way, he tried to provide for me, but couldn't fully. I suppose I'm still looking for that from you. I do know the paper's interesting."

Following this session, Kenneth had a severe bout of diarrhea. In the next session, the therapist empathized with Kenneth's feeling of devastation and his rage at the therapist for not being the father he wished him to be. Exploration of these feelings led to connections with Kenneth's other relationships, especially with his bosses, who all eventually disappointed him. His characteristic response to this was maintaining an air of superiority, distance, and withdrawal. Kenneth came to realize that his preference to do isolated research rather than working with a team led by a chief engineer stemmed from avoiding his anticipated frustration in a relationship with a boss.

Gradually Kenneth's attitude toward the therapist changed. Kenneth idealized him less and was able to express some criticism. Complementarily his dreams reflected a growing self-esteem: "I was looking for an old battered station wagon, but it was gone. I found a new blue wagon. I had a key and tried it, and it fit. I opened the door, hesitated, and closed it. Then I opened it again and drove it. Maybe it was really mine. I drove it down the road. I felt content." A second dream during this phase was: "I was peeing, and it was a huge, thick stream, and it went a long distance." The dream expressed Kenneth's growing self-assertion as well as the feeling that he was expressing his anger toward the therapist, and toward others, more directly.

Group was suggested to Kenneth after eighteen months of individual treatment. Kenneth had recognized the defensive quality behind his need to withdraw from others and had come to identify elements of both positive and negative transference reactions to the therapist. He had struggled with the disillusion of his idealized image of his therapist and had made substantial beginnings in separating out from the therapeutic symbiosis. The working alliance seemed firmly established and sufficiently flexible for entry into group.

Kenneth's actual entry into group reactivated fears and anxieties he had had at earlier attempts at individuation. Although he denied undue anxiety and looked forward to the experience, Kenneth had the following dream before his initial group session: "I'm in a small hotel, and the elevator is stuck. There is a narrow stairway, however, going to the sixth-floor meeting. I wasn't sure it was important but I wanted to go anyway. I walked up about to the first landing and then back down. My wife was there, and I asked her if she still loved me because I didn't know if I had the courage to go up the stairs. She nodded, and I walked back up."

Kenneth's associations to this dream revealed intense anxieties; he feared individuation yet felt that relationships could trap him. "I won't wear a wedding ring because I fear it won't come off. As a child, I wouldn't climb through drain pipes at construction sites with other kids for fear I would get stuck in the middle." He then associated to his first "conscious emancipation," recalling his mother removing a baby harness in his carriage and his resultant freedom to move about. He liked that freedom, but was also frightened that his mother wouldn't be there for him if he went off on his own.

Kenneth had gotten beyond a lifetime pattern of mistrust and distancing, denial and projection. Primary in this progress had been the very individually attuned therapeutic relationship, a process much more likely to occur in individual therapy. At the point Kenneth was ready for the addition of group, his ambivalence about his separation and his self-defeating defensive maneuvers needed to be worked through, and the group would offer added power to that endeavor. In the combined analytic setting Kenneth would be exposed to a range of emotionally laden responses not available in his individual treatment situation. A heterogeneous group of men and women would help Kenneth work through conflicts and problems that he had identified in his individual sessions but continued to struggle with. He was also still intensely ambivalent in his relationships with women, and had difficulty in empathizing with others or communicating feelings. He needed to gain in self-confidence and to venture into competitive situations with men.

Kenneth's initial reactions in the group fluctuated between

genuine interest, with some idealization of the members, and intolerant, hostile feelings, which he hesitated to admit. He generalized his negative feelings about himself to the group at one stage, saying, "We are a bunch of dolts."

In the group Kenneth was experienced as pompous, passive-aggressive, and competitive. His humor sometimes amused people, but they also responded to the aggressive and sadistic elements that were essential to it. Kenneth's puns were revealing; a favorite was, "What do you call a sadistic gardener?" with the rejoinder, "The Marquis de Sod." The group members came to accept the jokes and to appreciate Kenneth's attempts to relate in a more relaxed, less rigid manner. At the same time they responded to the defensive aspect of his humor, his attempt to gain control over powerful figures, including the therapist, by devaluing or demeaning them in order to feel less helpless himself. In Kenneth's individual sessions the therapist related this humor to the "dolts" Kenneth felt his parents were and the "dolt" that Kenneth had internalized and acted out. The therapist identified and empathized with the vulnerability connected to Kenneth's doltish feelings and also spelled out what the effect of the defensive-aggressive aspects of Kenneth's humor was on other group members.

Coming to understand the anger he sometimes elicited in the group served to help Kenneth differentiate the feelings his character traits provoked in others from reactions generated directly by the distortions of others. The therapist spelled out these differentiations in the individual sessions using experiences he had observed in the group and then made similar observations in the group. Ultimately, the group's capacity to understand and work with Kenneth's defensive communications and his ability to process their feedback paved the way for improvement in his interpersonal involvements.

The decision to add group is never clearcut; rather it is a weighing of the positives and negatives. As treatment progresses, the positive indicators for adding group increase to the point where the therapist makes the decision to go ahead. There will be limitations as well as advantages imposed on the therapy by this decision. The limitations are primarily in terms of the ending of a consistent, open, and empathic quality that individual treatment promotes, which is least inclined to evoke defensiveness from the patient. Adding group always results in some increase in defensiveness, some increase in anxiety, and frequently temporary regression. Nevertheless, the long range benefits of the group in effecting working through and change justify the decision.

CHAPTER 3

The Transition: Preparing the Patient for the Group and the Group for the New Member

A New Phase of Treatment

Entering group, and the preparation that precedes entry, mark the beginning of a new phase of the treatment and the end of the exclusive individual therapy relationship. These changes and the anxiety that always accompanies them make the transition a stressful period for the patient. The therapist must be sensitive to the complexity of the process in order to facilitate the transition. The special collaboration that is required between the therapist and the patient during this period deepens the working alliance.

Individual therapy has prepared the patient for entry into the group and the combined phase of treatment. The patient has understood the connections between his or her history and its psychodynamics; major characterological defenses—ego-syntonic—have been noted and explored. The transferences to the therapist have been observed, noted, and worked with in the individual sessions.

If the treatment has been productive, the patient has experienced changes by this time. The patient is better able to cope with relationships, and intrapsychic conflicts have been reduced. When conflicts occur, they are more likely to be effectively resolved.

Underlying these changes is the development in the relationship between patient and therapist. The process of understanding the anxiety dilemmas that brought the patient into therapy and placing them in the context of a life history fosters a strong and intimate relationship, an amalgam of positive transference and a working alliance. This relationship is a dynamic interaction, conscious and unconscious, between patient and therapist.

The case of Kenneth (chapter 2) illustrates the importance of the work done in individual analytic therapy as preparation for the transition to combined therapy. At the point of transition, the therapist felt he and Kenneth had reached a solid working relationship. This gave the therapist confidence that Kenneth would be able to work with the confrontations his provocative attitude would inevitably induce in others in the group. The fact that all this had been spelled out in his individual sessions made it possible for Kenneth to tolerate the group's response. He was able to experience fully and in a new way the impact of his passive-aggressive defensive stance.

The preparation for Ellen's entry into the group had another set of considerations. Ellen, a woman in her late twenties, had been seriously anorectic in her teens. With the aid of extended psychiatric treatment, she retained only the residuals of the condition: an exaggerated anxiety at gaining ounces beyond the spare weight she maintained, and about wanting more than one glass of wine in the evening. The psychiatrist Ellen had been in treatment with previously was described as a kind but "no nonsense" person who, Ellen felt, treated both the anorexia and later her inclination toward excessive drink as weaknesses that should not be tolerated. Indeed, he had helped Ellen to a much more balanced state.

Since the serious dangers of anorexia were no longer a problem for Ellen, there was now the opportunity for more exploration of Ellen's formative years. Her first dream in this treatment was of approaching her mother and having her turn away. Memories and associations to the dream led to a reconstruction of a very lonely, emotionally isolated childhood with older parents. Ellen's mother had been depressed and emotionally unavailable; her father had worked long hours, sometimes through the weekend, and was physically not there. As the therapist reflected an empathic comprehension of this, Ellen began to feel understood. For the first time she began to talk freely about how odd and deviant she had always felt. Her words for herself were "creepy" and "wimpy." This process continued. By the time Ellen entered group, she had acknowledged her craving for a nurturing mother. She was aware of how, unconsciously, she was enraged at the subtle rejections she had endured. She now felt less of a deviant and could work on issues related to sharing the therapist with others.

The Transition

Adding group is meant to deepen further what has been experienced in individual therapy. The therapist helps the patient understand his usual defensive maneuvers in the group setting. Characterological defenses will evidence themselves. Group therapy will offer the patient the opportunity of a broader field for self-experiencing and for understanding any resistance to change. The group will be a part of the process of working through and termination.

In his two years of individual analytic therapy, Alex had come to understand the origins of some of his feelings of grandiosity, his unrealistic expectations of himself, and his intensely critical attitudes toward others. He was a very intelligent research scientist, but ambivalent about his work in a highly competitive industry. Though he felt "safe" with his wife, he recognized how critical he was of her. Alex stated that he wanted to change these behaviors, but was also aware of how he clung to the safety of feeling superior to and disdainful of others. This attitude had been important in his relationship to the therapist until, as he put it, she could prove she was at least as smart as he was. When combining individual and group therapy was suggested, Alex was interested. He quickly agreed that the group might be helpful for exploring his apparently unchanging attitudes toward others. In the next individual therapy session, he reported he had been having two fantasies about the group. One was that he would take it over and become the leader, that no matter how competent or smart they were, he would be the best. The other fantasy was that the group would "rip him to shreds," that no one would like him, and that he would be destroyed. His underlying fears and his characteristic defenses were spelled out in that fantasy.

The therapist's suggestion of adding group may elicit a variety of emotional responses. Frequently there is increased resistance in whatever mode is characteristic for the patient. The patient who can block and deny will stop recalling dreams and suddenly find that there is nothing to talk about in the session, whereas people who tend to get flooded with anxiety report feeling shaky or having somatic symptoms again. This can strain the working alliance and may generate negative transferences toward the therapist.

When his therapist first suggested to Stuart that he might benefit from combining group therapy with his individual therapy sessions, Stuart's immediate response was, "That's fine, no objections." Stuart was passive and unable to express directly any opposition to authority, and habitually avoided and denied. The therapist heard Stuart's usual defensive style in his all too easy agreement and commented on this, urging Stuart to consider what his response really meant. If this had not been attended to, Stuart's response to what he experienced as being pushed would have been increased passivity and oppositional negativistic behavior.

Often there is an increase in anxiety in ordinary everyday life experiences. Some patients report feeling that they have slipped back to a more troubled level of functioning, more like the way they felt at an earlier time in treatment. Here the therapist educates, telling the patient that entry to group frequently evokes these reactions and communicating an understanding of the patient's experience. In the individual session, details of the group entry reaction are linked with other times the patient has felt this way. Gradually, the patient will tolerate the anxiety of the new therapeutic situation, understand and integrate the feelings and memories it activates, and gradually move on to new growth experience.

The differences in how the patient fantasizes about entry into group have important diagnostic functions. For example, Helen tended to idealize the group as a place for the reflection of her own needs and values, seeing the group only in positive terms. Many narcissistic patients deny any possibility of anxiety, projecting the fantasized "all-good mother" on the yet unknown group. In contrast, Amy took her usual masochistic position that the new experience was going to be a disaster. One of the best diagnostic signs for entry to the group is the patient's capacity to be in touch with ambivalent feelings in the therapeutic relationship. Helen was aware of her positive and idealizing responses to the therapist and also of her resentments and competitive feelings. She felt anxious about entering group but in confronting and working with that anxiety, expanded the whole treatment process.

In the ongoing individual sessions, patients need time to fully explore and analyze the reactions set off by the therapist's recommendation to enter group. New hope and curiosity will be stimulated, but at the same time, the therapist's suggestion of group will arouse anger, fears and mistrust of the unknown and anxiety about the group's response. Both sides of the patient's ambivalence will be expressed directly or indirectly through dreams, associations, and acting out in the treatment. Some patients will begin to question whether therapy is of any help at all. Others will feel they urgently need more time, an additional session a week. The therapist, though convinced of the importance of combining analytic treatments at this time, listens to the patient's resistance as it is expressed. The therapist may be aware of some individuals or situations in the group that will provoke negative responses in the patient. The therapist will know that a patient like Stuart will inevitably have problems dealing with an Irene, who is very much like his wife. So the therapist will ask Stuart how he thinks he would react to someone in the group who tends to be critical and provocative.

In the individual session, the therapist focuses on memories of earlier experiences with groups, starting with the family and relationships with siblings. Peer group experiences growing up are revived and linked with current social and occupational group situations. The increased awareness that results from sharing information helps to focus the patient's attention on what might occur in the transition into group. The therapist and the patient are then able to use this focus to make the transitional period more productive, as they anticipate what the impact of entering a group might be.

Ellen had gone over the history of her childhood experiences as the deviant in the group. She was the only Protestant in her class in a Jewish neighborhood school, and the isolation she felt, a function of ethnic differences, added to the strain of being the youngest child of aging parents. One evening, during the period of preparation for entering group, she returned to her therapist's office to pick up an umbrella she had left there. Walking into the waiting room and encountering a group of people there, she experienced an intense burst of anxiety and ran out of the office. Discussing this later in her individual session, she quickly connected it to the feelings of the earlier school situation. As the therapist was Jewish, she quickly assumed that the group was mostly Jewish and that she would be the deviant again. Ellen was afraid that after struggling for many years to feel part of a group, she would lose that good feeling and the accompanying confidence in herself. Her anxiety about going into the group had mushroomed; surfacing these feelings and memories was crucial.

It is a questionable issue whether a patient should enter a group unless he or she can consciously accept the plan and be able to explore the unconscious meaning of the experience through dreams and associations.

Valerie's struggle with her intense anxieties about entering a group was revealed in a dream she quickly connected to her conscious fears and the anxiety she had been feeling. In the dream, her cat was crossing a dangerous highway to get to a diner on the other side. Once there the cat stopped at the door.

The place was full of aggressive, snarling cats. The cat pulled back frozen in terror. Valerie recognized her fears about entering the group in this dream. She had frequently symbolized very personal feelings through her cats. Recalling and associating to the dream helped to reduce the intensity of her anxiety.

A generalized anxiety dream is frequently produced early in the transition period. Heinz Kohut describes fears of loss of self or self-cohesion, which may be symbolized in dreams of losing teeth or hair (1977, 109). Other patients with more flexible, well-developed self-systems may express in their dreams their ambivalence about entering the group. For example, one patient dreamed he "got off a bus he had been on to return to his own car."

The process of moving from an amorphous fear of the unknown, to understanding its origins and its defensive functions, to integrating its conscious and unconscious meanings, is the essence of the transition process. The integration and mastery of some of the elements of the initial anxiety is evidence of strength of ego functioning. Moving from diffuse, unfocused anxiety to ambivalence indicates that the person is ready to use more adaptive defenses and integrate new understandings into total functioning. The move from the knowns of the individual therapy to the unknowns of the group situation draws from new levels of self-organization and mastery.

Using Family Drawings to Prepare for Group

The period of preparation and transition from individual therapy to combined treatment may take several weeks. As part of the preparation, the therapist asks the patient to make a drawing of his primary family and bring it to the individual session. The instructions are presented simply to patients to make a drawing of their primary family on a sheet of 8 $\frac{1}{2}$ × 11 paper. To questions about when and how, the response is, "Whatever you like."

Patients usually react with surprise and disbelief. Making a drawing is different from anything they have experienced in the therapeutic relationship. It is a unique experience to have the therapist assign a task to be done outside the session. Like any disruption of the consistent framework of the sessions, it stirs up anxiety. However, it is a useful stirring up at this point in preparation for the whole series of disruptive changes that will be experienced during entry to group. Patients react with characteristic resistances to being asked for the drawing—they avoid the task, forget to do it, or do it perfunctorily. Many express shame about the drawing or apologize for its quality. At the same time the patient is often amazed by the memories and experiences, not quite unconscious, that are evoked by the drawing. Patient and therapist collaboratively look at the resistances and the origins of transference reactions as they are seen in it.

Anna, a conscientious and orderly young woman who was always a most cooperative patient, forgot to bring in her drawing for weeks. To date in her treatment she had been prompt for sessions, paid her bills on time, and remembered dreams. At first Anna denied that she was annoyed at being assigned drawings. She disowned any conscious reasons for the delay. Finally, after weeks, her good intelligence and her expectations of herself in the therapeutic alliance led her to admit that it did seem she had some resistance to performing the task. Anna had to recognize this to go ahead with it. Immediately following this exchange she did the drawing, and was surprised by what she produced, quickly linking the result to her resistance to the task. In the drawing she had positioned herself, the younger of two daughters, as a child between both parents but closer to the father, with the mother looking away from her to the older sister. Holding on to the father, the child Anna looked warily at the mother.

Anna recognized that being asked to draw had upset her because her usual intellectual controls would not be operative. She was aware intellectually that the feelings expressed in the drawing were all known to her, but apparently she had not really integrated them emotionally. Anna's associations to the drawing led to an increased understanding of her anxieties about entering the group. She had had a strained and angry relationship with her mother in the past, and this had softened. Her experience in therapy had provided a relationship of trust and intimacy in which she had gradually modified the transferential expectations she had had of thinking she would not be understood or approved if she were to reveal her inner feelings. The prospect of entering the group had reactivated her transferential fears. Anna was afraid she would lose her newly gained social comfort and return to an isolation she had lived with so long.

Another patient, Marjy, drew a simple line drawing of her two parents together, on the upper side of the page, and drew herself below, tending the baby brother in a baby carriage. She had poignantly and simply presented both her experience of the distance and the absence of both parents and her defensive response to this, which was becoming a caretaker and providing her younger brother with the nurturance she so craved for herself. Again, this relationship had been intricately explored as it emerged in treatment, but the drawing crystallized and emphasized it. The therapist had discussed with Marjy the likelihood that she would assume this role in the group, as it was the characteristic role she had taken in other relationships. In the group, Marjy revealed the nature of her family drawing after being repeatedly challenged for taking on a caretaker role and never directly dealing with her own issues.

The Patient's Experience

From patients' reports as well as from clinical observations, we have learned about the intense anxiety of the transition period and how it affects the behavior of patients in the group and in their individual sessions. Dreams prior to and directly after entering the group provide additional validation of the complexity of this experience.

In the individual session the patient may avoid or deny the stress of the transition. Some bring to the individual session a torrent of response to their first session in the group. For example, patients may report, "I was so shaky I couldn't say anything," or "I was afraid I'd burst into tears," or "How could I expect them to understand my problems; they're so different," or even, "What made you think that would be helpful to me; they're so sick." Understandably, the patient brings his anxieties and upsets back to individual therapy because of the established working alliance, and will not be comfortable so soon with its extension into the group.

The patient's experience of stress stems from both the impingements on the analytic relationship as it extends into the group and from the impact of entering the group. We will look first at the disruption of the exclusivity of the patient-therapist relationship. Psychoanalytic writers have stressed the complexity and intensity of the patient-analyst relationship as being the core of the therapeutic process. Winnicott (1971) has characterized it as a holding environment, while Mahler (1975) has stressed that in its earlier stages, particularly for the more narcissistically damaged patients, the recreation and reexperiencing of an earlier symbiotic relationship is extremely important. Modell (1976) has described how in the earlier stages of the analysis the patient and the analyst identify to an increasing degree, and this identification forms the new object relationship developed by the patient.

Whatever the terms, there is a powerful reciprocal involvement, conscious and unconscious, of patient and analyst. That it will be jolted by the transition into the group seems apparent. Still, many patients may try to deny this, to keep the connection unaffected. The therapist needs to remain aware of how difficult the transition into group is for the patient, as well as for her or himself.

As for the impact of the group on the entering patient, Freud's (1955) and Bion's (1961) descriptions of the possible regression of the individual in a group are still applicable. Entry into a group can arouse primitive fears and anxieties. These feelings are heightened by the contrast to the powerful feelings that can be experienced in the individual session as a function of unconscious merging with the analyst. Transferential reactions emerge that are different from those present in the individual sessions (Durkin 1962). In addition, there are the ubiquitous family transferences stimulated by the group, which are not present with the same intensity in individual therapy (Kadis 1956; Wolf and Schwartz 1962).

The experience of Agnes in making the transition illustrates many of these issues. A single woman in her thirties, Agnes had been in treatment twice a week for more than two years when the recommendation for group was made. She was a beautiful woman, a working actress, who had come to therapy concerned about the relationships she had formed with men. She had had a series of extended relationships, but something always seemed to go wrong and she ended up feeling exploited, hurt, bewildered, and very lonely. Agnes was also concerned about career problems as she was considered merely average talent in her casting agency. However, she was well aware of her apathy and that she didn't fully use the opportunities that were available to her.

The oldest child in a large, lower-middle-class family, Agnes had grown up feeling isolated and lonely. She always felt she was a burden to her mother and was unable to compete with her younger sister for her father. At school she conformed, dutifully obeying her strict teachers, but her fine intelligence was muted. In her fantasy she was a princess, a fantasy that was indirectly supported by the attention her unusual good looks brought her.

Compliant, beautiful, perfectly dressed and groomed, Agnes smiled frequently. The smile did not reach her eyes. She was more doll than woman. Agnes experienced anxiety somatically as a shakiness, an inner trembling, a rush of heat, or a sudden feeling of cold. At the same time she would experience increased apathy.

Agnes had made substantial changes by the time group was recommended. She had become more natural, more assertive and less likely to deny reality, withdraw into fantasy, or feel victimized. She had initiated a new career for herself and was gratified with her competence in it. In her relationship with her therapist she was more natural and self-consciously assertive, but continued to be inhibited about expressing either love or hate feelings. Through dreams, these feelings would enter the session and be acknowledged, albeit distantly.

Agnes had a better understanding of her relationships with men. She recognized the rage she felt underneath her over-compliance and her anxiety about relinquishing control. She began to see the role she played in setting up relationships that never led to the kind of commitment she claimed she wanted.

The therapist recommended group for Agnes for a number of reasons. She felt that group would help Agnes experience and express transferential feelings in relation to the therapist more directly. A group would also provide some corrective emotional experiencing for the angry, distant, non-communicating family ethos she had grown up in. And it could provide her with the opportunity to receive some honest information about her impact on others.

Agnes, as expected, agreed to the suggestion that she enter a group. In the following individual session she reported intense anxiety dreams about losing all her teeth. She recalled her experiences with groups. She remembered feeling strained, defensive, lonely, competitive, and resentful in her family. These feelings continued until she left the house. It was not until she returned as the successful sister who had moved up into a different socioeconomic universe and was able to provide gifts and know-how for her younger siblings that she experienced some change.

As a child outside the home, Agnes had felt only marginally accepted. She had felt unable to cope with the toughness and aggressiveness of the kids in her neighborhood, but managed to conform enough to be allowed to join the fringes of the group. She felt that the other girls envied her good looks, assumed the boys were only interested in her sexually, and wanted to keep her distance. In adult life Agnes managed to make a new group of friends, but maintained her distance by playing the role of someone very fair, reasonable, ready to carry her share of responsibility, who would ask for very little. Inwardly she felt resentful, frequently hurt, and very unsure of herself.

In her family drawing Agnes placed herself between her younger siblings, at a distance from both parents, looking nondescript like the other family members. She wore slacks, in contrast to the skirt worn by the sister who was her father's favorite. There were no connections indicated between any of the family members; they all looked straight ahead, nobody touching or reaching out to anyone.

On entering the group, Agnes was her usual perfect-looking self, smiling ingratiatingly. She was back to an earlier defensiveness in manner. The group members were all polite but distant. In part it was their reluctance to include a new member, but it was also a specific reaction to Agnes, one that she elicited. It was different from the reception accorded other new members. In the second group session Agnes said that the group "feels so warm and accepting." To Agnes's surprise the comment was met with suspicion and discomfort. At that moment there was a good deal of tension and resistance in the group, and Agnes's denial of it distanced her further. As group members expressed some of their wariness to her, she began to pull back and to bring her complaints about the group to her individual sessions. She was angry and felt that the other women envied her and that the men were intimidated by her.

In the group Agnes remained anxious and stilted. The therapist encouraged Agnes first in the individual session and then in the group to try to stay in touch with her feelings of being excluded and uncomfortable. The therapist was more active than usual in the individual sessions to fortify the therapeutic relationship, which was clearly being strained. In the group Agnes was tearful at some confrontations, and the group members became more aware of the defensive aspect of her behavior. The therapist intervened in the group by interpreting some of the defensive aspects of Agnes's stance and encouraging her to tell the group of some of its origins.

Agnes gradually began to build her own working alliance with the group. A few months later she was able to deal with the surprising information that the men in the group had felt distanced by her manner rather than attracted by her very good looks. Agnes was jolted and felt shaky but was not defensive when she learned this. She worked in her individual sessions with the pain and sadness of her emotional neediness and her role in perpetuating it. She began to feel comfortable and comforted in the group as she became able to use her real kindness and sensitivity in interacting with other members. She realized that their responses to her were based on real attributes of her personality.

Unlike Agnes, for whom the timing of the transition worked well, Frank's case makes it clear that the point at which a patient is ready is not always apparent.

Frank was in his early thirties. He had been in treatment for a year-and-a-half, three times a week, and had made remarkable progress. When he had come to treatment, he was a very pressured, anxious, obsessively preoccupied, but successful businessman. He was involved in a great deal of social activity with men and women that had a false, unrelated quality maintained at considerable cost by the use of cocaine, alcohol, and clowning.

At the outset, Frank was ready to hand over all authority to the therapist. He quickly developed a strong positive transference and then gradually started to participate in the analytic process, albeit in a fairly passive manner. Frank moved ahead to establish what seemed like a good and resilient working alliance. Reconstruction of his history revealed a childhood in which he consciously identified with an ineffectual mother who was browbeaten by a sadistic, immature father. The father habitually undermined Frank and was resentful of the mother's attention to him and his younger brother. Less consciously, Frank identified with the irrational explosive aspects of his father and was terrified of this. As he grew up, Frank had withdrawn from both parents. The result of this was an intense disorganizing anxiety and little sense of himself. He performed poorly at school and was shaky and self-conscious with peers.

In the process of reconstructing his history, Frank began to feel more self-respect, was less intimidated, and much less anxious. He started to change the masochistic, exploitative relationships he had set up with women. The recommendation that he enter group was based on a number of considerations: the idealized transference would be more effectively dealt with in the group; the obsessive preoccupation with himself and his problems would be interrupted if he could engage more in the concerns of others; and the therapist, a woman, felt that interaction with the other men in the group would add an important dimension to the treatment.

Frank had an immediate, intensely negative reaction to the suggestion that he enter a group. He had only miserable memories of life in his family. He had felt continually frightened, powerless, and humiliated. At school he had felt fat, stupid, and unable to compete. The therapist had hoped that the reality of the group response to him in the present would provide a corrective emotional experience to combat the persistence of the negative feelings rooted in the past. Frank agreed to join, with the proviso that it was only a trial and not a commitment.

In the group he sat silent and tense. Back in his individual sessions, Frank reported feeling terrible in the group. He was disorganized and anxious, a way he hadn't felt since before he started treatment. He saw no reason to go on with the group; it just felt like too much. But Frank agreed to attend a few more sessions as long as the therapist understood that he would not continue beyond that. Reactions to the group that he reported in subsequent individual sessions were generalized intense anxiety and discomfort with no focus on individual people or content. After five weeks, Frank withdrew from the group.

Though Frank was unable to work in the group at that time, the experience proved useful to the work in his individual therapy. There was no interruption of individual sessions, and Frank continued to move ahead. The confrontation with the therapist and her acceding to his decision seemed to improve the collaborative quality of the working alliance. It was important to Frank that he was able to assert himself, win, and still be able to continue a working relationship with the therapist. The quality of Frank's relationships with friends, both men and women, became more open and honest, and his chronic tension and anxiety continued to diminish. He became much more relaxed with the therapist, and was able to joke and have differences comfortably.

A year-and-a-half after the experience with group, the patient asked if there were currently a space in group as he was now ready for it. After some exploration of the previous experience and the changes in him since then, Frank entered a group. It was not the same group, but similar in quality to the one he had been in (men and women, twenty-five to forty-five, intelligent, all within the neurotic range, all functioning in their careers). Frank quickly moved into an active and productive participation in the group. When questioned by group members about his previous experience with group, Frank said that he had entered at the therapist's recommendation a year-and-a-half ago, but that he had not been ready for it. He clearly enjoyed telling them that he had differed with the therapist and had been proven right.

In retrospect, Frank *was* right. The quality of his relationship with the therapist at the time could not tolerate the addition of group therapy. It threatened the inner cohesiveness he was building and thus its therapeutic effectiveness. Frank had been working on very early issues of organizing and individuation, which required a kind of fantasy merging with the therapist for therapeutic progress to proceed. When recalling his early childhood, he remembered seeking to protect himself by pulling the covers over his head. During this period of treatment he experienced the therapist as his benevolent grandmother, and thus as a powerful supporting person. The group became an intrusion.

With more understanding of this phenomenon, the therapist might have avoided the error in timing. It is important that the therapist remain open to the patient's communications so that they can make decisions collaboratively and that any errors in timing can be corrected constructively.

Preparation of the Group for the New Member

Group members are affected by a new patient entering the group. The transition period, when the group composition is changing, can bring to the surface significant associations for each individual in the group. It is important to prepare the group to receive the new member. The period of preparation provides useful therapeutic material and enhances the therapeutic process for all.

In one group, the announcement that a new member would

be entering was met first by silence and rueful expressions, and then annoyance at the therapist for breaking into the good balance currently present in the group. In recent weeks group sessions had been particularly pleasant. The therapist realized that there had been a notable absence of critical comments or hostile feelings in the group for some time. He raised questions in the group about this, suggesting that it seemed unnatural. Further exploration gradually revealed that the group was so gratifying lately that members had selected to hold back on negative feelings or comments. Their individual resistances to bringing up disturbing material had been supported by group resistance, an implicit collusion to keep things pleasant, which the therapist had also been caught up with. When the resistance was revealed, two members then brought up issues they had avoided talking about for the last few weeks.

Under optimal conditions, the analyst gives the group members time to share their fantasies, expectations, and thoughts about the new member. This period, which can last three or four sessions, can generate significant individual therapeutic work in the group. Recollections about the birth of new babies or other early changes in the family constellation may emerge. Some group members recall when grandparents came to live with the family, while others recall older siblings leaving. The preparation of the group is related to the state of the group and the group issues as well to individual intrapsychic dynamics. The entrance of a new member will cause some breakage in the intimacy of the group, so members may want to share material that is particularly sensitive before the new member arrives. Often new transference reactions emerge, resistances to intimacy in the ongoing group may surface, and new material may come to the fore. Once these are analyzed, time should be left to deal with the issues relating to the new member.

The Transition

Since all of the group members are, or have been, in individual therapy with the group therapist, fantasies about the patients they have seen in the waiting room often occur. When there is an announcement of a new member, this may elicit more fantasies about the therapist's other patients. Wishes, preferences, likes, and dislikes are explored, and the meanings of these fantasies and projections become important. At times they are indirect expressions of what an individual patient feels is lacking, what the therapist is not providing for him, or what the group is not giving him.

Nan, who was very competitive with her female therapist, said, "I hope it's that older man I sometimes see in the waiting room. He looks so kind and understanding. I know he'll understand me." Joe said, "I hope it's not that woman who looks so depressed every time she comes out of your office. Who needs that?" Sue would say, half joking, whenever a new member was announced, "Maybe now you'll introduce me to Mr. Right."

Some patients reveal their fears of being displaced in the group by the new member through an intensification of dependency needs expressed primarily in their individual sessions. There may be a regression and an accompanying wish to solidify their special bond with the therapist.

It requires time to work with the complexities and changes that occur in the group whenever the arrival of a new person is announced to the current group members. The fears of displacement and possible new demands, the anxiety about "having to repeat it all," and the wishes for someone who might magically supply what had been missing are anticipated changes to be explored before the new person arrives. The various fears and anxieties are reworked when the new member is finally in the group.

The therapist will also have thoughts about the new addition to the group. How will this particular new patient affect the balance of the group? How will the new patient respond to the group members, and vice versa? At the same time it is important for the therapist to be alert to less conscious wishes. Like the patients, the therapist may also be hoping that a new group member will supply something missing in the group. The reality of the new person—his or her particular characteristics and ways of behaving—will affect the group dynamics.

When the therapist said that a new member was to join the group, Max's hope and fantasy was that it would be a woman, "Preferably attractive—I could use some stimulation here." Max was a young man who grew up in a household with three sisters, an overprotective mother, and a narcissistic father. While he preferred to be with women, he was subtly hostile and undermining in his attitudes toward them. Divorced, he could not maintain an intimate relationship, though most of his friends were women. He had worked on many aspects of his mistrustful and oppositional qualities in relationship to his male therapist.

The women in the group were offended by his remark about needing some stimulation. They tried to understand why he devalued them. He always seemed to be wanting "something better to come along." This led to work on Max's discomfort with intimacy within the current group; the competitive and provocative aspects of his statement in terms of other men in the group; his wish for the analyst to feed him with attractive women; and his desire to reverse roles with his father by becoming the center of attention. The prospect of a new group member reactivated many of Max's conflicts.

Another member complained that the new person would be an intrusion, and was annoyed at the therapist for it. The group would have to review the group history for the newcomer. The therapist acknowledged both the anxiety and the real annoyance at the intrusion of a stranger. He then asked if people could recall their own experiences of entering the group. This led to various members recalling the differences between then and now, and to some review of group history, which made them able to recall their own anxieties on entering the group. It was now possible for them to feel more empathic with the unknown new arrival.

Others in the same group had different reactions to Max's remark. Vernon, a rather compulsive thirty-four-year-old businessman, noted how much Ann, a forty-year-old divorced businesswoman, had changed. She could now handle Max's implicit devaluation of all women, while some months ago she would have been caught up in an angry tirade. Now she could reflect on his motives while letting him know how put-off she was by his self-indulgent fantasies. Ann agreed with Vernon and felt she was able to be more tolerant with Max, who could no longer "hook" her into a transferential need to prove she was okay with a teasing father who would ultimately devalue her. The therapist recognized the origins of each group member's response to the new person in the member's own history. Knowing the history of each individual in the group, the therapist is able to work more effectively with the fears and anxieties evoked by a current situation.

The group theme then moved back to change and the new member. One of the other women, Hannah, said, "I thought of a man coming into the group, probably married and depressed. It wasn't my hope, but I couldn't come up with a hope." Her depression was clear to the other members. Upon reflection, Hannah recalled that her fantasy about the man emerged right after Vernon seemed to be complimenting Ann. Hannah wished she could draw such compliments, and felt enraged that Vernon reserved his depression for her and his seductiveness for Ann. This in turn paralleled her feelings about Max's fantasy about a new, attractive member and her feeling devalued by him in the group. She used Max's wishes to fuel her own sense of hopelessness and her recall of her father's sporadic, seductive attention, which could never be relied on.

The preparation of the group can encourage exploration of the intrapsychic transferential meanings of the impending change. Once these are considered, identified, and worked on group members are in a better position to deal with the task of integrating the new member into the group as they continue to work on their own conflicts and transferences raised by the new experience. The therapist, by adequately preparing the new patient and the group members, has strengthened his working alliance with each.

Some therapists do not inform the group in advance that a new member will be joining them. They argue that it maximizes transference reactions and serves as "grist for the mill." The therapist who prepares the incoming patient but not the group may not be sufficiently attuned to the needs of the other group members. We believe that not working with the group in preparation for the change interferes with maintaining the working alliance. The unannounced new member can induce severe envy and jealousy among the group members and intensify negative transference reactions to the therapist for creating confusion or displace them towards the new member.

When the group has not been prepared for the new member, they may also react to the implied disrespect from the therapist. Not announcing a new member until his or her actual arrival is inconsistent with the collaborative quality of the working alliance the therapist has established with each of the patients in the group. The discrimination between the induced reaction to the situation and the intrapsychic fantasies of the patient is better achieved when there is an adequate preparatory phase.

When planning to bring a new person into the group, the therapist should be mindful of the current state of the group. When a group is in the midst of working intensively on one or several important themes, the arrival of a new member might be too disruptive. There are times, too, when the emotional tenor of the group would not make it possible for the group or the new person coming in to work productively. Because the group process is complex and various individual responses to and experience of both the anticipated and the actual arrival of a new member supply a great deal of material for the group to work with, the therapist need not add unnecessary or additional ingredients to this process.

One group therapist immediately replaced a patient who had left the group with another patient he had been preparing for some time. The group had not dealt with the loss of its old member when it was abruptly confronted with a new one. The new patient was met with extreme hostility, which neither the therapist nor the other patients really understood. Exploring his own involvement, the therapist became aware that he had unconsciously tried to ward off his anxiety about the loss of the member by creating a replacement. One root of the therapist's anxiety was a primitive transference fear that the group members would deal with their separation and loss by directing their rage towards him. The new patient became a target for this rage, serving as a scapegoat, and had a difficult time working out an initial alliance with the group. The group in turn had unified around the recent loss and had few resources left to communicate a sense of empathy for the new patient's difficulties, let alone his anxieties in a new situation. This example indicates that the therapist's own countertransference reactions may be a factor in not preparing the group for a new member. It illustrates the importance for each therapist to maintain an awareness of his or her contributions to the process.

The therapist's role during this transition phase needs to be evenly balanced between considering the intrapsychic issues raised by the introduction of the new member and the task of dealing with group resistances to the reality of the impending change. When group members focus solely on issues raised between them by the new member, to the point of denying the impact of the group member on their therapy, the analyst needs to interpret this. Otherwise a group can escape into intellectualized rationalizations such as, "This is none of our business," or "We understand there should be no problem," or "Okay, let's get on with our stuff," and set the stage for isolating the new patient once he arrives on the scene.

The analysis of the change in the total gestalt of the group and its impact on the individual takes priority. It is the quality and intensity of these reactions that are important, not their existence. For patients who are vulnerable to narcissistic injury, the time of each entry of a new member to the group is a valuable opportunity for additional working through. The disruption of the gestalt allows for increased awareness of narcissistic issues.

Initial acceptance of the new member is frequently expressed by group members' reminiscences of their own difficulties in entering the group—the fears, the awkwardness, and the experience of being a new member and an outsider. For the group this acceptance promotes a feeling of valued communality. For the new member it generates hope that the present discomfort is transitory and will soon pass.

The entrance of the new patient often stimulates dream material among veteran group members. This material becomes part of the continuing preparation of the group as well as useful clinical material for enabling the working through of significant intrapsychic conflicts in ongoing group and individual sessions. The state of the working alliance is also reflected by the capacity of patients to share their dreams in the group after the entrance of a new member. We feel it is a positive sign when a veteran patient shares a dream related to the new member with the new member present, and less of a positive sign if the veteran tells it only in the individual session. The latter may be an indication of splitting of the transference or of other resistances and may strain the combined analytic working alliance.

In an individual session after a group in which a new woman member was introduced, Mary shared a dream. She was in the back seat of a car with another female patient. The car was driven by her family physician and two women, one of whom was the new group member, were in the front seat with him. They all shared the secret of having an affair with the physician, except for her companion in the back seat. Notably, the men in the group were left out of the dream.

The analysis of the dream revealed the impact of the new female patient in Mary's old fantasies of having been displaced in the oedipal triangle and the narcissistic blow of having to take a back seat. It also raised her denial of negative feelings and her secretiveness. Indeed, Mary tended to compartmentalize her feelings and was uncomfortable working in detail with this dream in the group. Transferentially, the group members became the disapproving parents. The working alliance had been strained, and the transference resistance had been temporarily elevated.

The therapist continued to work with Mary's resistance in the individual sessions. He accepted her reluctance to discuss her feelings about the new patient in the group sessions at this particular time. The therapist's careful interpretations enabled Mary to understand, slowly at her own pace and without the pressure of the group, the transference resistance and repair the working alliance. Eventually Mary was able to reveal her competitive feelings toward the new woman in the group, working through her sibling and oedipal rivalries in the individual and group sessions.

Bringing in dreams at a new member's first session can have several meanings. It can be a statement that it is "business as usual," not letting the new person interrupt the ongoing process. It can also be an expression of trusting the new member with personal communications and may be experienced as a statement of acceptance and inclusion. It is also an implied expression of trust of the therapist and of the strength of the working alliance.

In another group, Bernice, who had a strong working alliance, easily shared a dream after the entrance of two new group members. The new members were Matt, a man in his fifties, and Grace, a young woman in her thirties. Her dream was: "A new Christian woman leaned over to the man next to her and the other women joined in. I was aware I had rejected the men because they were not the men I would choose, and they were having sex. It looked very casual and good, and it was some kind of revelation."

In the group, Bernice, who is Jewish and in her late forties, associated to Grace's ability to attract the attention of the men in the group. She associated Christian with "not like me" and gave some memories of women she had observed as a girl when she went to the beach with her mother. She had not shown her mother how interested and envious she was of the freedom of these "bad girls." Bernice went on to describe how she devalued the men in the group as a defense against dealing with her natural impulses. The revelation was that sex was good. Bernice and the group members subsequently worked on the historical sources of her underlying anxieties. Indeed, Bernice always seemed to appear controlled and inhibited and until recently had preferred conjoint therapy, where she could maintain the split in her behavior.

In the group, Bernice was able to work on transference reactions stemming from early family experiences which were evoked by the two new members. Reactions related to her husband were stimulated by Matt. They both were in the same profession and of similar age.

In this group situation, the therapist encouraged Bernice to work on the genetic meaning of her dream. Since she was comfortable enough to present it in the group at this time, he felt she could do this. The therapist also worked with Matt's and Grace's reactions to Bernice's dream. When a dream that has been stimulated by the entrance of new members is presented in the group, it is useful to help the new members respond to the dream.

The introduction of new members can influence the intrapsychic life of group patients and serve the ongoing therapeutic process. For the new patients, Bernice's dream and the work with it helped introduce them to the unique value of the group therapeutic process. Their reactions were worked on in depth during subsequent individual sessions, and continued in relevant areas during group sessions.

The Therapist's Perspective on the Transition Period

The therapist facilitates the transition period by modulating the anxiety of both the new patient and group members to a tolerable level. Interventions are directed first at maintaining the working alliance. The new member needs to experience that the working alliance experienced with his analyst extends into the group; at the same time the group members need to reaffirm that their working alliance with each other and with the therapist will not be superseded.

The therapist is likely to make a nonverbal acknowledgement of the new member—eye contact or a nod of the head —as the group enters the room. However, no verbal intervention is offered, permitting the group to proceed as usual, to start their exchanges, initiating the process for the session. If there is more hesitation or restraint than usual, the therapist may intervene to facilitate the group's start: "It's hard to proceed when there is a new person in the room." The group may take this as an indication to proceed as usual or address the new person.

The new member in the group intensifies the involvement with the therapist of both the entering patient and the other group members. The transition evokes a heightened experiencing of anxieties related to competition with siblings and peers and its accompanying anger and dependency. It is likely that the group resents the intrusion of the new member. The transition to group brings some additional correction to remaining idealizations of the therapist and with this, some of the anger and disappointment that accompany it. All of this impinges on the therapist.

The therapist notes the unconscious expression of members' feelings in the various forms of resistance they express. Sometimes group members will act unnaturally cooperative and "therapeutic" or peculiarly silent or irritable and curt. The therapist's intervention will aim at their resistances, commenting, for example, on "the unusual number of therapists in the group tonight," or "How hard it is to talk about private things when there is a stranger in the house."

The Transition

In the meantime, the therapist has his own new perceptions. There is always some surprise at observing the patient, seen heretofore only in individual sessions, in the context of the group. The new data gained by observing the patient interacting with others change the picture for the therapist. Frequently the transference has slanted the patient's behavior in the dyadic sessions to compliant, awkward, or unsure roles. This same patient may show social coping skills or ease on entering the group that are quite different from the way he or she has been behaving with the therapist.

In her individual therapy sessions, Pat persistently described herself as "stupid, ineffective, and incompetent." Although a graduate student in literature, she felt inadequate and reported that she never participated in class. In her work in individual therapy, she focused on her helplessness, reenacting in the transference her earlier relationship with her mother. Pat's mother was a self-absorbed women who could respond to her children only when they seemed in desperate need.

From her first group session, Pat's behavior was very different from the way she had interacted with the therapist in her individual sessions. The other group members' expressions of their needs evoked a mature responsiveness in Pat. She proceeded to demonstrate a competent aspect of herself that had only been suggested in the individual sessions.

The therapist was "surprised" by the change in Pat and was alerted to the countertransference-transference deadlock that she and Pat had unconsciously perpetuated in the individual sessions. She was then able to facilitate work in the group that clarified the history and dynamics of Pat's defensive limitedness.

The experience of Pat's functioning in the group, the feedback from group members, and the therapist's increased awareness of her own unconscious countertransference enabled the group to confront the meanings of Pat's view of herself. This was important for understanding the transference—Pat's repetition of her way of relating as a child—and its function in the evolving resistances to change.

Group members' responses to the patient which are apparently at variance with the therapist's frequently signal the possibility of some countertransference reaction. This will be clarified as the group members' surfacing transference reactions to the new patient are explored and compared. For example, one therapist was not completely aware of the extent of a patient's provocative behavior. The unanimously negative response of the group to his cutting remarks and derogatory comments alerted the therapist to her countertransference aroused by the patient's cleverness in his comments about persons or events. The therapist's enjoyment of the patient's wit did not allow her to anticipate how, uncontrolled, this might be used defensively by the patient in group.

Another example of "surprise" when the patient enters the group was the experience with Mitchell. Mitchell, an intelligent, boyish-looking young man, tended to be restless, self-conscious, and mannered. He had formed an immediate intense attachment to his woman therapist. Mitchell brought to the relationship unconscious expectations of the intense merged relationship he had with a very volatile, assertive mother, who adored him, hovering over all aspects of his existence. In the dyadic therapy Mitchell quickly engaged the therapist, discerning her interests and her sense of humor; he trusted her completely and uncritically. When the therapist would note any of this, Mitchell smilingly agreed. He began to understand some of the transferential aspects of his relationship to the therapist, responding easily and eagerly to interpretations. As therapy progressed, he became more aware of characterological defenses and the origin of these in his developmental history.

Entry into the group was particularly difficult and anxiety-provoking for Mitchell, an only child who had always had strained relationships with peers. He was totally in agreement with the plan to include group in his treatment, but was concerned about it. He was excruciatingly aware of a lifetime of misery with peer groups, where he had always felt uncomfortable and unable to function effectively. As a result he was even more anxious than usual, and the entire defensive picture was magnified.

At Mitchell's entry to the group, the therapist was surprised to see how inappropriate his behavior was. Mitchell whistled as he entered the waiting room; the jokes he told were unrelated to what was going on. He also turned to the therapist in the group with personal asides of an oddly intimate quality. The therapist became aware of the complementary countertransference she was involved in with Mitchell and was struck with the realization that she had unconsciously colluded with the patient, responding uncritically to some of his impulsive, exhibitionistic moves, as his mother had done. With her own and the group's awareness of this and responses to it, the therapist and the patient began to work this through in the group and in the individual treatment sessions.

The new expanded awareness of the countertransference sharpened the therapist's perceptions and permitted corrections and modifications. Such countertransference distortion of the therapist may exist at a very subtle level. Ralph Greenson has observed that the patient's desire for empathy modulates the amount of empathy evoked in the therapist. Heinrich Racker's "Law of Talion" is congruent with this; that is, there is a tendency for the analyst to respond to a positive transference with some positive countertransference and to a negative with some negative countertransference. Therapists are human, affected by how people feel towards them. Frequently they reciprocate subliminally, and the countertransference only surfaces when confronted.

Individual treatment permits the therapist to carefully time interventions that challenge a particular defensive stance, gearing these to the patient's tolerance for difference. But in addition to the therapist's conscious accommodation, there tends to be some margin of unconscious adaptation to the patient's particular sensitivities.

Paula, an unusually conventional woman in her thirties, had profound doubts about her value as a person. This was coupled with extreme discomfort with her sexuality. She tended to assume a rather arch, pretentious manner in her interactions. In the course of two years of individual therapy the therapist had become so accustomed to this that it often went unnoticed. With Paula's entry into the group, the therapist again became more acutely aware of it.

When Paula first participated in the group, the response to her was an uncomfortable silence. Restrained, careful comments were voiced, some echoing her tone. Gradually there was a decided difference. The group began to offer plain, direct, and natural communication, contrasting with Paula's distancing stance. The therapist was reminded of her own initial reaction to Paula's persona and realized that it had gradually come to be ignored as irrelevant in the dyad. Yet this persona represented crucial defensive issues for Paula, who assumed that hiding herself from observers was the best choice considering the inferiority of what was underneath the facade.

As in the case of Mitchell, the therapist was able to use this heightened awareness of Paula's defensive stance, in both individual sessions and in group, to promote change. The therapist's capacity to remain open to the corrections the group provides is crucial. It can make this transition period into an important development of the therapeutic process. The collaborative exploration in both settings leads to a new strengthening of the working alliance.

The following example further illustrates the complexity of transferential and countertransferential issues that a therapist has to deal with during the transition period.

Simon, the new member, had met the group in the waiting room. Bea and others had warmly welcomed Simon, but once in the office the group ignored his presence. Max took center stage, engaging the group in a detailed discussion of something which had occurred during the week. Despite occasional interruptions, Max persisted. The therapist became aware of his reluctance to intervene and gradually realized that he was involved in a countertransference reaction induced by Max. Max had made it clear that he needed the new member to be a woman, one who treated him better than Bea did. This induced in the therapist a feeling of being the bad mother Max was experiencing. As the therapist became aware of this and its inhibiting effect on him, he was able to make the appropriate intervention. He noted that the group was acting as if Simon weren't there. After some acknowledgements of this by other members, Max said that he indeed felt competitive urges, especially when he heard the positive quality of Bea's welcome, that he defended against by ignoring Simon. Max was then able to acknowledge Simon's presence and address him. Simon set off in Max the negative feelings like those toward his father, whom he experienced as competitive and depriving.

The multiplicity of issues evoked by the patient's transition make it apparent that the number of individual sessions should stay constant during this period. Experience has shown us that it is not in the best interests of the therapeutic process to reduce the number of individual sessions at the same time as the patient enters group. The patient may feel that the therapist is being arbitrary in this decision. The therapist may need to explain the rationale for it and hold firmly to it, though sympathetic to the patient's concerns about the additional time and/or money. This is another step in the whole transition process which can deepen the collaborative aspect of the working alliance. There is a change in the total gestalt of the therapeutic relationship because group is added.

Once the transition has been made, the initial anxieties confronted, and the patient has extended the working alliance to include the group therapy context, then a reduction in the number of individual sessions can be considered.

Summary

An established working alliance and a therapeutic relationship that has explored both positive and negative aspects of the transference are required for the patient to navigate the transition to group successfully. Careful timing is important for the new member as well as for the group.

This period of transition from dyadic to combined treatment is a complex one for both patient and therapist. In most cases it leads to an expanded and deepened awareness for both that will bolster the process of working through issues first formulated in the individual phase of therapy in group. These issues are reexperienced and heightened in the transition to group and continue as the patient goes on to the combined phase of therapy.

CHAPTER 4

The Working-Through Process

I N psychoanalytic treatment, "working through" is the most ambiguous of clinical terms, yet it refers to the critical task of treatment: the translation of understanding and insight into change. It is this phase that determines whether the therapy has been essentially effective, whether symptoms have been relieved, emotional responses and attitudes have been effectively altered, and new behavior patterns have begun to develop.

Working through can be defined either in terms of its goal, "a stable change of behavior or attitude" (Greenson 1967, 29), or in terms of the recommended procedures, "the repetitive, progressive and elaborate explorations of the resistances" (42). In either case, the difficult task for the patient and the therapist is to get beyond the persistent repetition of old neurotic patterns.

The combination of group and individual therapy is an ideal context for this "essential constituent of analytic work" (Fenichel 1976, 463), which consists of "rediscovering what one has found in one place in many others." The addition of the therapy group expands the therapeutic field and includes a broad range of additional stimuli. In the group, a variety of personalities impinges on each other in a unique fashion. The truth of insights the patient discovered and explored in individual therapy is repeatedly verified in a variety of situations. The established relationship with the therapist facilitates reexperiencing these in the new context of group. There is profound trust carried over from the individual analytic work, and with it a resilient working alliance and a shared awareness of both positive and negative transference reactions.

The patient and the therapist have shared information from the individual sessions that is brought to the work of the group directly and indirectly. In the individual session, the therapist may work with the interactions from the past group or anticipate a coming group session. When David, for example, had avoided telling the group about the recurring depressions which had brought him into treatment, the therapist commented on this in his individual session. David said he did not feel ready to talk to the group about this, not knowing how, and not being sure he would get a sympathetic response. The therapist asked if he wanted help in bringing it to the group. David's immediate response was "No. I'll do it when I'm ready." It was clear to the therapist that David would consider it a betrayal, not helpful, to reveal anything about his depressions in the group until then. Two weeks later in the group session, David began to talk of how much better he was feeling but how depressed he had been in the past.

In contrast to David, Arnold, a very passive man, asked in his individual session whether the therapist could help him get started in the group. Though articulate, Arnold could not speak up in the group. He never knew when it was the right moment to interrupt, or how to get to what he wanted to talk about. The therapist observed that this really was a central problem for him and a crucial goal in his therapy. Arnold agreed, but asked if the therapist could help him. The problem of his passivity needed to be worked on in the group. But first Arnold needed to form a strong working alliance in the group as a context for this, and he needed a great deal of attention and support from the therapist in the group. With this initial help and the feedback from the group, Arnold could begin to identify the meaning and origins of his defensive passivity.

The climate of the group is uniquely familial. Developmental sequences are recapitulated in combined therapy because of the sequential transition from the dyad to the group; that is, the intimate, exclusive relationship with the therapist developed over time in individual therapy is brought into the larger group. At that point the therapist's relationship with other people is evident and open to examination for the patient. This expanded view of the therapist and of one's self in relation to the patient evokes anew old feelings.

Intense sibling rivalries are experienced at first usually with patients of the same sex. For some patients, however, who experienced a no-win situation in their families with the preferred opposite sex sibling, the group evokes that same response. Whatever the particular pattern, the move into the group situation triggers off in an immediate and intense way old family constellations. But just as in the individual session, the patient had the corrective experience of not getting the anticipated response to certain behavior. In the group the patient does not get the familial reactions anticipated. Inevitably there will be some people who respond the way family members did to the patient as the product of evoked transferences. However, there will also be those who are not caught up in this way whose responses will be free of the patient's history.

For the therapist, too, the climate of the group adds a new dimension. The spontaneity of group interaction challenges the "role playing" therapist. The give and take demanded in the group requires flexible and authentic reactions from the therapist. With the opportunity to step back and observe the patient in interaction with other group members, the therapist gains a new perspective. In the dyadic analytic relationship there are many aspects of the patient we do not observe or learn about. The therapist gets a new perspective and can correct whatever merging there has been with the patient's point of view. Observing it, the therapist becomes aware of his or her own countertransference reactions, and this sharpens and broadens the total analytic process.

In the group the therapist is necessarily more exposed, behaves more spontaneously, and is watched more closely by some patients. Facial expressions, bodily postures, and other nonverbal cues become very important. Group members also attend to the therapist's interaction with other group members. This may set off sibling rivalries and the consequent rage or complaints towards the therapist is expressed directly or indirectly in the group.

It is important for the therapist to have had some experience in group as a participant to be aware of how he or she responds in group situations and to be more prepared to deal with member comments. Because these responses are intensely transferential, they arise quickly and powerfully, and the therapist needs to be aware of personal behavioral inclinations in order to sort out perceptions of the real interaction from the transferential exaggeration.

One group member accused the therapist of stiffening, like his mother, every time he became angry and raised his voice.

The Working-Through Process

He felt he had been set up, encouraged to express feelings, and then been dealt "the silent treatment" of disdainful disapproval. In this instance it was important for the therapist to know, from her own experience as a group member, how apparent her strong response to loud, angry voices was. She could then sort out from this the transferential meaning the patient gave to her behavior. She did not have to deny the action, but could help the patient deal with its possible meaning for him.

Clinical experience verifies the observations throughout the literature that the process of working through can be difficult, frustrating, and tedious for patient and therapist (Greenson 1967, 88; Karush 1967, 512). Effective emotional learning takes time and effort. It requires trying new ways if patterns that have existed for a lifetime are to be altered. Participation in a group can promote this. Group members provide encouragement and motivation for continued efforts. Positive responses to new behaviors can reinforce their efforts and increase the probability that neurotic responses fixed by history will be modified. Most important, the group provides the opportunity to deepen and amplify insights as they are revived and reexperienced empathically in parallel concerns with other people's lives.

The group permits a person the time to be silent as changes within are experienced without feeling a need to put them into words. Productive working through for patients in a group may take place while they are listening to someone else articulate issues they respond to profoundly themselves.

There are times when a patient may communicate nonverbally with the therapist. As Peter was talking about his overprotective, over-generous, but belittling father, Anne looked at the therapist, nodded, and smiled. She was communicating her knowledge that she and the therapist both knew that Peter's experience would be helpful to her. In her individual sessions, Anne had complained that she would not be able to fit into the group. The familiar feeling of being a misfit had been her initial response to it. Now she recognized what she shared with Peter. Listening to him tell of struggles with his father allowed her to develop a new repertoire of responses to her own struggles for recognition and self-esteem.

The therapist and the group members may also communicate nonverbally to the group. Group members may notice and make a particular group member aware of the fact that whenever he or she speaks it involves looking at one special person in the group. Whom group members address, where they face when talking about a particular problem, can all be understood in the group in terms of the implied communication. Group members may also be particularly attuned to the therapist's gestures or changes in posture and bring it to the group's attention. In one group the group members were able to point out to the therapist that they could tell when she was going to offer some particular interpretation. They noted that she tended to lean forward in her chair, tucking her hands under her as though to increase her forward posture. With this nonverbal signal, they would then wait for what was coming or, as one member noted, if he felt it was something he didn't want to hear, he could "run interference" and leave no room for the therapist's intervention. For the therapist, who was only minimally aware of this postural change, it was a useful observation. Its very accuracy left her with mixed feelings: she recognized how true it was, acknowledged the intentions behind her postural shifts, and also felt a little self-conscious about her nonverbal communications.

Frequently the therapist and the group do not learn of the impact of a particular session on a group member until later.

The Working-Through Process

A patient, Frank, told the therapist in his individual session and then announced in the group that he had felt "wiped out" by the previous group. Both the therapist and the group were surprised. Frank had said little during that session. His facial expression had not been revealing. In fact, he had not appeared involved at all. Natalie had been talking in the group of her complete helplessness coping with the university hierarchy, which had slowed down her research for eight months. She could not proceed with her graduate work because the faculty was blocking her and she had no recourse. As she talked, Frank reexperienced the complete impotence he had felt in his childhood. These feelings still surfaced periodically, particularly in current encounters with women. When he was blocked or feeling unable to negotiate, he would become silently enraged and completely unable to remain in the interaction with the other person. Listening to Natalie gave him an additional perspective on his own recurrent and overwhelming experience and he could now understand it in a different way.

How Working Through Proceeds

Group sessions usually follow the same general routine. The first few minutes usually represent the changeover from the social conversation that was going on among group members in the waiting room away from the therapist, to the more authentic and introspective mood of the analytic process, where role playing, "maintaining a social front," is not valued. As the group settles in, one of the members usually begins with an account of some troublesome event or feeling that occurred during the past week and is persisting. Sometimes it is a residue of the last group or individual session. We believe that the much debated question of whether focus in the group should be on the here and now is a false issue. In all therapy, history is never recognized as relevant unless something in the present is setting off its residue; tracing its origins may then be helpful.

Because the session begins with a present occurrence, the account is frequently a story or a description of an incident or an experience that "threw" the speaker, causing unreasonable upset. In telling the story, the narrator gives cues to involvement by vocal tone, facial and body expressions, and defensive stance. Group members' first responses tend to be their characteristic defensive positions. One person needs more precise information; another has an immediate solution; one has a value judgment of moral repugnance; others can be disinterested, uncommitted, or have total empathy with the person who has been speaking.

Alfred, a middle-aged man who had been a member of the group for a number of years, was intense but also amusing. He used both his intellect and his charm to maintain control. Although Alfred was responsive and engaging, his intense jealousy and his need to control periodically surfaced in group sessions. When he was displaced in his role as the "wise, paternal figure," he became devastatingly sarcastic.

One evening Alfred was clearly agitated and said he must talk. He had found a letter to his wife from a man she had been involved with in the past. Alfred suspected that she had been receiving phone calls as well. He had read the letter. He could not tell exactly what was going on, and he felt as though he was going to go out of his mind. Alfred told the group that he felt he could kill the guy, and obliterate her. He had already figured out how he would initiate divorce procedures. Viola, who tended to automatically accommodate to the needs of any man she was with, quickly responded to Alfred with sympathy, communicating concern and caring. Joan, who tended to be angry at men and had difficulties finding one who could meet her standards, quickly identified with Alfred's wife. Joan said, "Hey, wait a minute. Haven't you been giving her a hard time lately, even before you found the letter? And how did you come to find it and read it?" she asked challengingly. In response, Alfred disclosed that he had gone through his wife's pocketbook. She had been out very late, and he was feeling uneasy about what was happening in their marriage.

Phil, who had a history of provoking women to leave him, became very excited and involved at this point in the group discussion. In the past, when living with women, he had set up "secret meetings on the side," constructing a triangle and acting out in fantasy unresolved oedipal issues. Phil hadn't acted on any of these fantasies for some time, but still found them attractive.

As the group continued, members got closer to the hurt and vulnerability they feared exposing in themselves, the relationships that they had seen as children and did not want to repeat. Alfred talked about how much his wife meant to him and his fear of losing her. He was aware of his urge to destroy when he could not control. The session had moved from "the presentation of a problem" to an awareness of certain anxieties and the defensive maneuvers used to cope with them.

In their individual sessions following the group, patients pursued their own responses. Phil looked again at his relationship with a controlling, distant father and the satisfaction he would feel whenever he would get away with anything. Joan renewed her awareness of her anger at men and examined her current relationship. Viola struggled with her readiness to merge and lose her own boundaries.

In his individual session, Alfred talked at length about his hurt, his anxiety, and his reluctance to bring up any of this with his wife. He never found the right time; fearing the confrontation, he avoided it. He anticipated rejection and abandonment.

Back in the group the next week, Alfred reported that he had been simmering all week, had withdrawn from his wife, but had not had time to talk with her about it. During this group session, the exchanges were more searching. Members were more related to their own conflicts impinging on their reactions to Alfred. The same feelings were there, but there was less tendency to immediately act on them. There was more observing ego present in the individual group members. They responded in their characteristic fashion—Joan felt angry, Phil was excited, Viola protective, and so forth, but the exchanges deepened and broadened as each brought in their own history and how it was impinging on the present moment in the group and on their current lives.

Alfred began to understand his wife's experience of him as group members told him how easily provoked he was in group and how difficult it was to explain things to him when he was angry or threatened.

In the course of the combined analytic treatment, an issue like this will recur in myriad different circumstances. The process of going through it again and again makes a gradual but consistent contribution to change. The person goes from awareness to real modifications in experience and behavior. Describing the function of the analyst in individual analytic treatment, Stephen Appelbaum sums it up succinctly: "What the therapist does is to help the patient to have in the present, through transference or recall, experience with roots in his past which are ordinarily unavailable to him in the present" (1981, 9). The addition of group sessions to the therapy amplifies this total experience.

The Working-Through Process

In one group, Hans and Victor repeatedly engaged in angry confrontations. Victor, the younger man, felt Hans did not respect him. Hans would move any exchange to only those subjects relevant to himself. Hans felt justified. At last he was emerging from his long withdrawn silence only to be interfered with and sabotaged by Victor who felt enraged by his behavior. Hans would repeatedly turn to the therapist to present his point of view. The repetitive quality of the behavior in both men made it apparent that a complex of transferential reactions was active, and that history known to both was being evoked. Hans was the intellectual older brother in his family. He had felt forced into a peripheral position by a talkative younger brother. Victor, on the other hand, had felt completely unable to compete with a brilliant older brother. The situation in group made them both recognize in the here and now that they had been repeating a crucial pattern of intense sibling rivalry. They knew these feelings historically, but had not fully realized they were operative in the present. Other group members had been lining up with one or the other, repeating characteristic reactions from their own history, and lending fuel to the conflict. Awareness of the transferential aspects underlying the present interaction helped both Hans and Victor to work more collaboratively in the group. They worked through important defensive reactions as related incidents came up again and again. Repeatedly tolerating and owning his own anger brought each man a step closer to integrating his awareness. The characterological defense, the feeling of being victimized, exploited unfairly, and being helpless was worked through.

The power of the group in combined treatment is in its evocation of intense emotional conflicts that call forth strong responses in everyone present. Experiencing intense anger and reacting to other people's outbursts of anger is a particularly valuable supplement to the dyadic sessions, where such exchanges are not usual for many patients and their therapists. The interventions by the therapist modulate the balance between experiencing the feeling and providing a context of historical understanding. The group setting provides the opportunity for both the therapist and the patient to experience "in vivo" behavior, which is often talked about in individual therapy. The group then provides a context for observing what evokes such anger and to understand it in terms of each member's own history.

In one group there was a periodic eruption of tension between two members, Leon and Barbara. He was an unusually intelligent and competent lawyer. She was an equally intelligent and talented writer. Both had many social skills, but both were anxious and easily threatened. Leon tended to feel safe when he was in control and not intruded upon beyond a comfortable distance. Barbara tended to lucid perceptions but expressed them in quips and off-hand remarks; "throw-away lines," the group called them.

In one session, Barbara felt particularly provoked by Leon's control of the group through subtle and sensitive maneuvers. She openly challenged the defensive posture he took about his own resistance to the therapeutic process. He said repeatedly in the group that no therapy was going to affect him significantly because his pathology was irreversible. He strengthened his argument by comparing his pathology to early religious training, which also remains fixed and irreversible. Leon and Barbara became angrier as the exchange escalated. He said he would like to smash her head in. She was outraged and bewildered, feeling she had done nothing to deserve this.

The therapist was aware that Barbara was particularly upset because of her response to the hopelessness Leon had expressed. It was something Barbara was struggling against in herself. Leon seemed to be both challenging and providing a voice for her feelings. The therapist decided to intervene with an observation of how intensely enraged Leon and Barbara were with each other and suggested that this was related to an issue common to both. Other group members became more aware of their own unexpressed feelings of hopelessness and their struggles with what felt so hard to change. Although their immediate responses to Leon were different from Barbara's, they could empathize with her anger towards him.

Explorations in the group and in the individual sessions led to an increased understanding of Barbara and Leon's anger but not to its diminution. Leon felt dangerously intruded upon by an unrelenting attacker. He felt "as if a knife were inserted and just twisted around in my heart." The history of his reaction led back to early experiences with a sadistic father. He had talked about it but had never experienced it as directly in the individual treatment. Barbara felt hurt at Leon's reaction. She was "just telling it as it was" and had no awareness of the impact she was having. She was surprised to find out that other group members felt something similar to what Leon had said. Encouraged by Leon's articulate presentation of his point of view, two other group members revealed that they saw her as provocative, tending to "twit" people. Amy felt the bite from Barbara's comments as "horseradish, a condiment that was sharp but really added to the dish." David experienced the precision of Barbara's barbs, but saw them as valuable rather than dangerous.

The therapist commented on some of Leon's negative transference feelings towards her, suggesting that to some extent it was being displaced onto Barbara. Leon denied that there was any more intensity directed at Barbara than appropriate for the quality of her attack on him, although he acknowledged that the therapist, too, felt intrusive at times but "more like a can opener than a knife." David said that although he didn't share Leon's response to Barbara, he did share the response to the therapist. Neither Phil nor Ellen could find Barbara's comments anything but amusing. They reacted to her humor and had no discomfort with any of the underlying rage.

The combined reactions of the group members provided all the necessary elements for Barbara to gain a real comprehension of how she expressed rage when she felt pressed or controlled. She learned about the effects of her behavior and its impact, and at the same time received sympathy and admiration, all within the context of a group climate directed toward understanding and helping.

The night after the group, Barbara had the following dream, which she remembered in her individual session: "I was in the house. It was dark outside. There were three people. Someone came to the window, and they were going to kill someone in the house. There was a feeling of being trapped in there and being very vulnerable. I went into the closet and grabbed something, went to the window, saw all those people, and suddenly it was a truce—peace—they weren't going to harm anything at all."

Barbara felt peaceful when she awoke and recalled the dream. She connected it to an interpretation offered by the therapist of an encounter she had had the previous week—that she projected her own rage to the world and then felt scared. She felt wonderfully calm at that moment.

The weekly group session provides a constant flow of fresh material as new responses are generated by group interactions. As group members develop complex involvements and attachments to each other, there is repeated opportunity for a new view of one's own concerns as they are confronted in group by others. People seem better able to learn about some of their own defensiveness when they are viewing it in others.

Resistance in Group

The primary responsibility for noting, confronting, and interpreting resistance belongs to the therapist. When there is ample opportunity for the resistant behavior to become evident in the group, the therapist may wait for the group members to deal with it. If the group members do not respond, the therapist will because it is the therapist's explicit role to deal with and analyze resistance as it emerges in the group.

The analytic group provides the ideal opportunity for the analysis of resistance because there are so many interpretations and confrontations available. Patients frequently tell us that they have come to understand themselves in the group beyond levels reached in the individual session, though they can't exactly explain why or how. One factor contributing to this is that in a group the patient can time his own interpretation. At the precise moment when the patient is ready to integrate and cope with an increased awareness, the interpretation is available as it is demonstrated or verbalized in some group member's parallel issue. For example, Martin listened to Letty's response to a younger woman in the group and could not contain himself: "I just heard myself as you talked to her; you were sounding so superior, so wise, like you knew better, and she's really foolish. Everyone gets so angry at me at work when I say things like, 'One would, of course, proceed in this way.' I really understood why just now."

Very often the complaints of husbands or wives become comprehensible to patients as they experience critical reactions to others in the group who display behaviors similar to their own. A man in one group suddenly said, "Now I see what my wife is talking about when she gets so angry with me. I avoid dealing directly with her the way you did to Sue just then. Boy, it got me mad just watching you." His empathic connection with Sue permitted him to have this fresh perception. With the help of the therapist, patients come to learn that intense discomfort evoked by another in the group is a signal that there is a similar dynamic in themselves, but possibly just out of reach of awareness.

Certain psychodynamic patterns are ubiquitous and come up repeatedly in group. One example of this is the patient who projects and denies and always perceives himself as the victim. Talking about this in relation to a mate, an employer, a physician, or a friend, the group becomes irritable. They begin to see the part the victim plays in his own victimization, and several group members confront him with it. Some confrontation comes from members who have come to understand this dynamic in themselves. But often the most intense irritation comes from people who are warding off or resisting awareness of it in themselves and deal with the resulting tension by angrily attacking the patient who acts as victim. The projective identification is masked by the fact that the group member they project on will also have the identical dynamic, but it is often revealed by the excessive intensity of their criticism. At the appropriate moment, it is the therapist's role to intervene and offer a clarification of the behavior of the member who is using projective identification and attacking.

For example, to John, who was attacking Marion's controlling behavior, the therapist said, "Marion's way of controlling by provoking people's guilt is easily discernible to you. We've seen you using the same procedure. It's hard for you not to at times."

Lois, who was usually a fair and accepting person, was extremely critical of David when he entered the group. She saw nothing positive in him and was annoyed that the therapist had added him to the group. Her reaction to David was extreme, contrasting sharply with her previous reactions to new members. It also differed from the reaction of other group members to David. The reaction was in part transferential—David evoked the feelings Lois had had to an older brother who tortured her in her early years and was their mother's favorite. David also evoked her feelings of rage toward men, her sense that there were "too few good men out there and more good women." As the hated older brother, David also threatened Lois's relationship with the therapist, who Lois had experienced as understanding and supportive. Now there were resonances in her perception of the therapist's relationship to David of her mother's attachment to her brother.

Along with the transferences evoked, Lois was responding to David's judgmental and contemptuous manner, a characteristic of hers which she did not acknowledge. It took months of dealing with Lois's responses in both individual and group therapy for her finally to acknowledge that she shared some of David's tendency to be judgmental and condescending. As she continued to explore the relationship to her brother raised by her responses to David, Lois got to the adoration she had felt for her brother as a child. She then could express her appreciation of David and feel some of the positive feelings she had toward him.

There is a truly facilitating effect in the acknowledgment by others in the group of a warded-off attribute in a member. For that person, there is relief in finding out that what seemed so disagreeable in themselves, a very personal "dirty little secret," has resonances throughout a room full of people who generally are accepted and valued.

In one group session Larry began to describe the sexually stimulating environment he grew up in. His parents encouraged nudity and open expressions of sexual interest between the children and between parents and children. Larry was troubled by his incestuous wishes toward his sisters. After he spoke of them, he was able to express his sexual feelings toward the women in the group. Other group members, freed by Larry's openness, talked about their own incestuous feelings and how this had inhibited their ability to express their own sexual feelings or fantasies about group members. Feelings of shame about childhood wishes and the repeated experience of shame as these were reexperienced in the group when they were shared, enabled the group to express a whole range of feelings that had previously been bottled up.

In combined analytic therapy, the group therapist is in a unique position to deal with resistances. Unlike conjoint therapy, where the patient has one therapist for individual treatment and another for group, the therapist who combines analytic treatments has a wealth of information about the material the patient presents to the group.

The therapist's associations to the patient's story in group are important. If a fragment of a dream or a piece of early history comes to mind, the therapist may choose to share his or her association at the time; may note it and hope that the patient, too, will make that connection; or may choose not to make any intervention in the group, seeing it as more relevant to the individual therapy work.

It is particularly necessary to reverse the traditional delineation of analytic roles, the patient as producer of associations and the analyst as interpreter. John Gedo points to the realization that as psychoanalytic therapy has moved from the authoritarian medical tradition, we had better appreciate that "the capacity of most patients to reach valid conclusions about the introspective data they produce in analysis has been generally underestimated" (1979, 253). Patients in combined treatment have an opportunity in the group to make their own connections and their own reintegrations independent of the therapist and the other group members. There is time and opportunity for them to be attending to their therapy autonomously.

In the group, the patient is more free of the analyst's bias in viewing his or her life and experience. Independently, the patient is aware of responses and avoids what can be a pitfall in the individual analytic session of verbalizing and formulating, forcing vague feelings or thoughts into words prematurely because there is a blank of silence to fill. In this sense, the patient is better able to work at a chosen pace in the group. The group gives a person more opportunity for silent contemplative experiencing. We respect the patient's freedom to use differentially the two modalities of group and individual as part of this more collaborative role.

Many times with sensitive issues where there is a just-dawning awareness, discussion is limited to the individual sessions for an extended period of time at the request of the patient. This is particularly true of feelings of shame, envy, or self-disgust. There can be therapeutic validity to the patient's choice to postpone introduction of the particular content to the group. The patient may not feel ready to cope with negative or non-empathic responses that might be evoked from other group members in the same area. It is important for the therapist to respect this. Pressing a patient to bring such material into group prematurely can create an intractable resistance in the treatment. We have learned that a group cannot be depended upon to time interventions or maintain consistent empathic response the way the analyst can in individual therapy.

The therapist may remain separate when untimely interpretations are offered. By simply remaining silent, the therapist can facilitate the denial or rejection of an observation from a group member. It will remain ambiguous whether the therapist agrees or disagrees with the interpretation. Usually there will be someone else in the group who will empathize with the patient's feeling of being accused or unfairly described and will turn the focus back on the interpreter.

A universal and poignant experience in analytic therapy is recognizing that the expectation of transformation is a fantasy. Past scars will be healed over but not erased, as history cannot be obliterated. In group, analytic patients help each other to come to terms with and relinquish their unrealistic fantasies about how analysis could completely transform them. Frequently they come to recognize their own hopes in another group member's struggle.

Frank had been doing well and feeling good, but then inexplicably had gotten into a bad mood. He discovered the key to his mood change in the group session. Frank had arrived at group feeling down. A combination of business problems and breaking up with his girlfriend reawakened early fears that he was "no good" and "would never amount to anything." Added to his problems was the disappointment that he was still vulnerable, that although he understood his early fears, he had not been transformed. In Frank, Fay recognized her reaction of a few months earlier when she had realized that though she had changed, she retained old imprints. She had gotten past this and reported a dream in which she was happily surprised to be celebrating her graduation; she was encouraging Frank while being empathic to what he was feeling. Other group members then shared that at different times in the past they had hoped they would be reborn, that their old or weak parts would be somehow lost, disconnected from them, and they would be starting fresh. Each had had some contact with the disillusion that has to come sometime in analytic treatment: the realization that one is going to be more oneself than not, no matter how successful the treatment. The goal is to help patients go on to a good feeling about the continuity in their personalities, rather than have them disappointed they are not being radically altered or becoming totally new people.

Another shared universal in group is patients coming to accept their parents as they feel stronger in themselves; they lose the feeling that unless their parents change, they will never be able to be adequate human beings. For many, this in turn leads to genuinely improved relationships with their parents, and discussion of these is frequent in the working-through phase in combined treatment. One patient announced to the group with humor, "Remember my old mother? Hostile, destructive, enraged? No more. She's completely changed. I'm amazed at how it's possible to talk to her now." Other group members concurred. "My father's more vulnerable and perceptive"; "She's less bitchy"; "He can hear," were implicit acknowledgments that getting beyond some of their own anger and demandingness had affected their parents and their relationships with them. Others in the group may remain skeptical or respond with envy or despair to the positive feelings expressed.

In psychoanalytic treatment change requires an alteration of patterns and involves a rewriting of personal history. In the group, members each work on revisions of their individual history. The dyadic phase of treatment gives them new patterns for organizing what they know of themselves and their history. Their task, however, is a complex one, and many missing pieces remain. Strengthening and filling in the new pattern is the task at hand, enabling patients to move away from the neurotic repetitions they had been involved in, and in which they had involved everyone they related to.

The Case of Elaine

A full report of one patient's experiences illustrates in greater detail how the working-through process is enhanced by the combined analytic therapy model.

Elaine was a young graduate student who had entered therapy because of marital problems. She had moved to New York with her husband, Peter. The couple was continuing their graduate studies, he in engineering and she in biology. The pressures of leaving their small Midwestern town and their families strained their marriage. Elaine and Peter had been at college together and had been able to help each other mask their anxiety at separation from their families by forming a close unit. Now in their move halfway across the country, as they tried to feel more independent of their parents, new problems emerged. Peter resented the restrictions of marriage; he felt "trapped." Elaine had always seen herself as a troubled person and felt that the increasing difficulties in the marriage were her fault. Her husband totally agreed with this view. She always blamed herself, and her marriage to a man who always blamed the other person made for perfect complementarity.

Peter agreed that if only Elaine would change, all would be well.

The therapist saw in Elaine an attractive young woman whose gracious good manners had an almost old-fashioned charm. She spoke well, choosing her words carefully, yet had a spontaneous quality as she recounted her history. As she noted how positively she was responding to this patient, the therapist realized how skilled Elaine was at endearing herself to people. She was moved by Elaine's story and realized that there was an openness and responsiveness in this young woman. At the same time the therapist made a note to herself to explore the role of the patient's need to please and her automatic compliance in her interactions with others.

Elaine had hoped to have a very different marriage from that of her parents. She had grown up feeling very troubled and had coped with her inner turbulence by forming symbiotic attachments to men in which she sought to comfort them in exchange for a sense of stability.

Elaine was intensely attached to her father. Growing up, she had felt that she had to make it up to him for the loneliness he experienced in his unhappy marriage. Elaine's mother was a deeply depressed woman who spent much of her time in seclusion. She was aware of and very jealous of Elaine's close relationship with her father. Using her fine intelligence and sensitivity, Elaine very early developed an ability to placate and calm this irritable man who was her father.

In therapy Elaine quickly became "the good patient," as she had been the good child. It became increasingly apparent that Elaine was usually compliant, rarely expressed differences, and that this quality in her relationship to the therapist would be central to understanding and interpreting the transference. This kind of "good patient" may initially be experienced by the therapist as pleasing and can be seductive. However, this has to be identified as transference so that it can have an impact on the work done in the therapy.

Early in Elaine's individual therapy she became aware of the deprivation she had experienced in childhood and continued to expect in the present. On the couch for the first time, she said, "I don't want to say anything. I have this fantasy that at some point I'll be talking and you are not in the room. I'd reach around for you and wouldn't find you. I'd be by myself." When asked to associate with the phrase "reach around," she talked about how both of her parents were really not there. She would "reach around" for her mother and realize she got no answers. This severely depressed woman would often be unable to answer her child's simplest questions. Elaine's father was often away on business trips. "I quit reaching around for them when I was seven or eight," she said. She went on to say, "I wonder if you want to be my mother," and then she added, "My fantasy was that you were scared when I said that."

Elaine had been convinced as a young child that she was responsible for her mother's depression and that her neediness was responsible for the mother's withdrawal. After bringing this information to the therapy relationship, Elaine had dreams that the therapist would not return from vacation because she had been dependent on her.

In the context of the individual therapy relationship, Elaine began to formulate for the first time the anger she felt at the way she had been treated as a child. She began to recognize, too, the depression she experienced each time she accepted the "blame" for any conflict.

In the first and second years of her analysis, Elaine was preoccupied with both her own poisonous, dangerous qualities and her need for "a mommy." She was very frightened of her dependency and her belief that the therapist would abandon her as soon as she knew how evil she was. The consistency of the analytic experience, with the therapist remaining neutral, empathic, and interpretive of Elaine's experiences, rather than attempting to gratify or reassure her, was the "corrective emotional experience" for Elaine.

The struggles with her fears of dependency and her fears of her own lethal qualities continued during Elaine's first two years of therapy. In her childhood, these fears and the unavailability of the parents had led to an exaggeration of the normal dimensions of sibling rivalry. There was competition between the four children for the meager parental supplies.

Repetition of the family patterns of competition and of the wish to be special were noted in Elaine's work and social relationships. It also was evident in the therapy relationship. Elaine had many fantasies about the patients who came before or after her whom she had seen briefly in the waiting room. The competitive feelings she experienced and her need for an exclusive relationship with the therapist were explored. The connections to her family patterns became increasingly clear as Elaine became aware of her fantasies about the other patients.

During the first phase of Elaine's therapy, the elements in her negative transference projections were identified, their genetic origins understood, and their defensive meanings revealed. The transference expressed her fears and her experience of abandonment by both parents. Even more terrifying for Elaine was the fear that if the therapist was caring, she would become consuming. Elaine responded with physical symptoms, choking, and asthmatic breathing when she felt the therapist was concerned for her or when she felt close to the therapist. Elaine was terrified by the feelings stirred up by intimacy with a woman. With men, she had felt able to seduce and engage them sexually. She felt helpless and at one time cried out in childlike rage, "If I had a male analyst, I wouldn't be going through all this." The therapist noted how fearful it was for Elaine to risk intimacy with a woman. She suggested that this seemed to be related to her mother's intrusive over-identification with Elaine.

Elaine amplified this observation, recalling how both parents had alternated between a closeness that became intrusive and excessively seductive, and rages and threats of abandonment that were evoked by any attempt at separation. These important experiences in Elaine's life were repeated in the transference in the individual therapy relationship. As these feelings were reexperienced and analyzed, the consistency and dependability of the therapeutic relationship made it possible for Elaine to come to trust the therapist and to proceed in building a more stable sense of herself. This enabled her to begin to deal with the problems around individuation.

Elaine came to recognize that her critical and competitive fantasies about patients she saw before or after her session were the same as her feelings about the siblings who had come before and after her. The second of four children, she had felt it was important to maintain a position of being "special." Although she intensely desired an exclusive relationship with the therapist, she was also very fearful of what this would imply. She would then have to be responsible for the therapist's well being. She was excessively watchful for any signs of fatigue or illness in the therapist.

As the genetic origins of these transference distortions were analyzed in her individual therapy and the working alliance grew stronger, Elaine became more aware of how these long-standing patterns of behavior were being repeated in many areas of her life. She began to experience some changes in her relationships with women friends and with male teachers. She found herself more trusting and less seductive.

When the addition of group was suggested in the third year of therapy, Elaine was fearful. The prospect stirred up old anxieties. She was afraid she would be rejected, that she would not be "the preferred one." She recalled that in school she had always been "the teacher's pet," but that then she would leave school to go home to loneliness and isolation. Sometimes she had had "a best friend." In high school her loneliness had been assuaged by having "a boyfriend," and in college she and Peter had quickly become "a couple."

The therapist suggested adding group to give Elaine an increased opportunity to work through some of these issues within the group therapeutic context. She reflected to Elaine her fear that there might be a repetition of her history in the group. The possibility that Elaine might feel increased anxiety was acknowledged, but group might enable Elaine to get beyond responses that were rooted in her history. The advantages would more than outweigh the difficulties that would be experienced in the initial disruptions of the strong dyadic relationship. The therapist was confident that Elaine could tolerate the increased anxiety of group at this time and that working through it would enhance the total therapy experience.

The intense anxiety and temporary regression induced in Elaine by the suggestion of group therapy were revealed in a dream. The dream and her associations to it give a sense of the upheaval she experienced, her awareness of it, and of her attempts to cope with it:

"It starts off visiting the office of a man I used to work with in Cleveland, named Joe. I was going to have an affair with him. In the office where we used to work, there was a bathroom. It was really an apartment, like this office. I took a shower to be clean and sweet-smelling. I'm in the shower and a woman walks in, a woman who used to work with me. She says, 'Look out, I'm going to get in, too.' She kept expecting me to respond in a negative way. This woman seemed to think that she was also going to sleep with Joe and maybe sleep with me, too. She expected I would be angry, but I wasn't angry. I took the shower. In the next part, I'm walking dressed in a lot of clothes, carrying baggage, with Joe and my father and brother, with a group of six people. We're walking miles to get where we have to go. We're going to my father's house. Everyone else is tired. What are we going to do now? It's not really as far as it seems. But we end up stopping in a motel. The motel is like a suspension bridge, and my father and brother and other people are in one part. Joe and I go on the bridge, facing each other. He reaches out to put his arms around me. The implication is he wants to make love to me. He said he was married. I didn't think he ought to. He ought to go home. He becomes angry and marches off the bridge. I begin folding up the shower curtain which used to hang in my bathroom. I was upset that he was angry, but I didn't know what to do. Getting off the bridge was scary for me. I have a strong fear of heights and exposed places. That's why I didn't want to make love on the bridge."

The therapist was accustomed to this kind of detailed-narrative dream. She was aware, as she listened, of Elaine's intense reexperiencing of recurrent emotional themes. The two images the therapist immediately noted were "clean and sweet-smelling" and "suspension bridge." They fully characterized Elaine's conflict and her alternating ways of coping. The "clean, sweet-smelling" child, an image of childish innocence, and the contrasting image evoked by the "suspension bridge," an image of precocious sexual excitement, were the persistent themes in the therapy. The anxiety of entering the group highlighted them again. The therapist was also aware of Joe as the "other man" in Elaine's life, a married man who represented the promise of a new symbiotic relationship; and was aware of the "long trip" as the therapy.

Elaine had reported many dreams in treatment and freely produced rich associations for them. In her associations to this dream, she noted that the woman getting into the shower looked like the woman who usually left the office just before she came into her session, "a small, sweet, gentle person." "When she's getting into the shower with me, it seems nice. Last year, when I used to come to the office, I had a fantasy that that woman was a lesbian. I've had a fantasy all week about the group. I have a lover now, and I expect if the group knows, they will be angry with me. I expect you to scream at me, to say, 'You have to stop.' And now I think she's going to take my lover. I wanted Joe to leave his wife. I felt a strong pull towards him. It was almost as though it was against my will. I was thinking about the shower curtain, too. Right after I bought a new shower curtain, something went on in my head about the shower curtain here. I had a fantasy that one reason I couldn't decide on the color of the shower curtain in the store was that I was getting confused with you. It should have been blue, like yours. I don't know what folding up the shower curtain means." The therapist, as always, attended to the transference message of the dream. Here Elaine's ambivalence was expressed in terms of the contrast between the "small, sweet, gentle person" and the "angry woman." The therapist followed Elaine's associations in this form.

The wishes for a symbiotic relationship that had been explored earlier in Elaine's therapy were evoked again by the prospect of entering group. An astute, observing ego was operating in her dream, anticipating the intrusion on the comforting symbiotic aspects of her relationship with her therapist. Elaine reached out, as she had in the past, for the comfort of a relationship with a man to repair the sense of loss and help maintain the inner sense of organization she was building. At the same time, she clung to the shower curtain, a symbol of her attachment to the therapist, but it was a thin, cold comfort.

The group situation, while it may evoke these clinging fantasies, at the same time provides protection against the fears of merging with the therapist. The hostile elements of these fantasies can be better worked through in the group therapy setting, where the level of functioning required by the group, the stronger ego defenses, allow the patient to tolerate the fantasies.

When asked to associate to the suspension bridge, Elaine said, "It's scary, but I loved it; it was exciting." She recalled the sensations she experienced when her father would come into her bed when she was little. What she felt as the bed moved—excitement, terror, delight—were all combined and very similar to the feelings she associated with being on the suspension bridge. The therapist was aware of the sexual excitement stimulated by the anticipation of group and particularly of the prospect of men in the group. Elaine's current feelings in therapy had triggered the recall of this early experience with her father.

Elaine went on with her associations, saying, "The suspension bridge in my dream didn't move. It feels like I'm isolated, and that's something very hard for me to deal with. The people I count on disappear. I feel very scared and very confused. The dream seems jumbled up. I can't think of anything to say. I think a lot about being dependent on other people. I'm afraid that I'll come to depend on a group of people who will, in the end, be taken away from me. It's not safe to be a person who needs." This is another illustration of the group serving to refocus issues not yet completely worked through.

Elaine's entry into group was a replay of what had been evident in her first individual therapy session. Her social graces, ingratiating behavior, responsiveness to other people's needs, and ability to create a climate around herself guaranteeing support and acceptance, were all present in the first group session. The therapist was able to watch how Elaine used her sensitivity to establish a connection to each individual in the group. She listened carefully for clues as to what different members of the group needed and seemed to anticipate complying with their needs. In the initial session she was not ready to express any of her feelings directly, other than her need to be accepted and safe.

In the individual session following her initial group session, Elaine said that she had at first felt a moment of panic when she had to decide where to sit, but then she felt really pleased about the group. She then returned to the dream. "I'm thinking more about the dream I had before I started group—the suspension bridge. I was scared when you started talking about the bridge. Many people jump off bridges. The dream had something to do with feeling that I will have to jump off here, that I will not be allowed, and that I will have to jump. It scares the hell out of me to be there with those other people. I felt glad to see you there. It reminds me that you're not the punishing person I think you are when I'm on the couch."

She then went on to talk about her fears of being judged, about the fact that the therapist would be angry with her, and would abandon her.

There was another dream after Elaine started in the group. "I came to group, and Lois was in the group. The two women,

Dorothy and Anne, are also in the dream. Also other women I don't know. [Lois was not a group member; Dorothy and Anne were in the group.] I think Bill was there, and the man that didn't come the first week. Eli came late. In the first part of the dream, you're sitting on the couch, but you're a man in your early thirties, nice-looking, well-dressed, not dressed in a suit and tie but with a beard—hip, very relaxed, with gold chains. But there's no question it was you. Lois was sitting on the floor at your feet, holding your hand and rubbing her face with it. It was a comforting and sexual thing. I remember thinking, how come she's that way with Lois and not with me? Lois is breaking rules here. Eli came in. I remember he was standing up. There's a kitchen behind the end of the couch. He looked so tall, and I felt so small. I'm delighted he has come. He's pouring himself something to drink; there's a terrible spill, a big mess. At that point, you were sort of directing everybody to sit down and make themselves comfortable. I was cleaning up the mess. I wanted something to drink. I put ice cubes in a glass, but I didn't see anything. There was a green bottle, but it wasn't really soda. I remember being so thirsty. The dream ended about then."

Elaine's associatons were: "Eli's like my father—very, very anxious, trying to make everything okay for everyone. I'm hoping he'll take care of himself and clean up his own mess. Lois—I'm not sure about that. There's something to do with the fact that I'm jealous that she might see you at the Center. I can't figure out why I put her into the group, especially at your feet. It's the position I'm in. I feel very sad. I feel I want so much from you." When asked about seeing the woman therapist as a man, she said, "It's easier for me. That game works, at least for a while. It's a dead end game, but it's a comfortable game. I have no tools to seduce you."

The Working-Through Process

Elaine went on to talk about wanting mothering, wanting the therapist to be her mother and resenting that she couldn't be. The specter of her depressed mother, though now better understood and appreciated, still colored her relationship with the therapist. "I have to please you, and I don't know how to do that." She could maintain a better relationship with the women in the group, she said. "I have good feelings about both women in the group, although Dorothy terrified me with her sadness." She talked again of her fears about the closeness which is threatening and, at the same time, what she wants.

Elaine's therapist was aware that the dream spelled out recurrent issues: Elaine's fear of abandonment, her wish to merge, her longing for mothering, her expectation of punishment, and her feeling that the only way to relate to men is to clean up their messes and take care of them. All of these themes had been worked on in individual treatment. Although Elaine had gained considerable insight and understanding of them, when she came into the group the old anxieties reemerged. She had intensely desired an exclusive relationship with the therapist, but was very fearful of what this would imply. In the group, she confronted the same fears about rejection, about being seen as crazy. The stress of the transition and the newness of the group situation induced regression: issues that had been dealt with previously reemerged in new and more intensified forms.

In the group, Elaine responded to other members as all good or all bad. The different men in the group were seen as either the good or the bad father, and women as the good or the bad mother. In a group, unlike in the individual therapy relationship, group members can respond more directly to those elements of the transference projections that don't fit. Thus, when Elaine accused one man of jealous possessiveness, he replied, "Sure I like you, but I'm not mad when you talk to Fred. I don't feel I own you."

For Elaine, another important aspect of the group experience was to hear other group members' transference reactions to the therapist. She was surprised to hear others did not experience the therapist as terrifying or destructive. As group members compare their varied responses to the same therapist, the complex interweaving of these responses with the transference reactions between members becomes an important part of the working-through process in the group.

As Elaine dealt with her old anxiety feelings that reemerged in group, she talked about the alternation of feelings of closeness and fear she was experiencing more profoundly as she faced coming to group each Wednesday night. Her longings for closeness were reawakened by the experience in the group. She kept waiting for something wonderful to happen, something like what she imagined it would have been like if her mother had held her. At first she had looked to members of the group for closeness and comfort, but came to recognize that she could not expect that from them.

After Elaine had been in the group for about two months, there was a surge of critical and negative reactions toward her. In her individual session she reported a dream: "I had a dream about you. I dreamt about you a week ago. I was angry at you. I dreamt I came here with two women. It was more like a board meeting. Nobody said anything. At the end of the dream you were making marks, like you were counting up people who were leaving, the patients, who were leaving." The dream expressed Elaine's disappointment with her group. She talked about the patients who were not in the group. She had hoped that some people she had glimpsed in the waiting room would be in the group. She had had very strong feelings and fantasies, both positive and negative, about them. When she recognized that they would not be in the group, she was disappointed. This became the focus for expressing her other disappointments with the group and with the therapist.

The dream allowed Elaine to express her negative feelings about what she was not getting. The therapist heard Elaine's expression of disappointment in the dream and her criticism of the therapist as judgmental and mechanical. She pointed this out to Elaine and commented that it represented progress for her to be able to express these negative feelings and reactions in the context of a dream. Hopefully, this was an indication that in the near future Elaine would be able to express criticism or negative feelings directly in her relationships.

Elaine then talked about her relationship with one of the men in the group and how seductive she had been with him. "It's a very easy way to be noticed. I can get angry and hide it in being seductive. There's a kind of anger that feels so sexy. But of course it ends up being a masochistic trap, and I'm depressed in the morning."

In the group, Elaine cautiously took on the role of caretaker, a defensive compromise she had frequently utilized in her life. This was an aspect of her behavior that she had talked about in her individual sessions. As it reoccurred in the group, the therapist chose not to confront it then, expecting that the group itself would get to it. This decision was based on the knowledge the therapist had about each of the other group members. Having worked with all of them in individual therapy, she could hypothesize about how they each might respond to a "caretaker" member. There were hints in their individual therapy sessions that for some of the group members this was becoming troublesome and arousing strong transferential reactions. Although the group initially enjoyed having someone who seemed to be there only for them, after a few months they began to question what she was doing.

Once the caretaker issue was raised in group, it was brought back to Elaine's individual therapy and the working through went on in both arenas. The confrontation proved to be a rich opportunity for Elaine to work through the defensive meaning of her "good mother" role. It had allowed her to deny and avoid competitive feelings with the therapist. She was too busy being a good girl and helping mother. The caretaker role also helped Elaine deny her wishes to be better than Mother. She had gained approval from adults in her life by being like them, identifying with them, and, as occurred with Father, in establishing an exclusive relationship with them that would make her special.

This caretaker behavior had reemerged in the group as Elaine's initial response to stress. As it was confronted and interpreted in both the individual and group sessions, it was gradually modified. In the collaborative effort of understanding the repetitive, compulsive nature of this behavior, it was seen as satisfying unmet developmental needs. Elaine's real sensitivity was then opened up to be used and shared in many ways which brought pleasure to her. No longer defensive, this behavior could become part of the autonomous ego. Once her infantile needs were worked through and the compulsive part of her behavior was modified, she was able to get responses from group members which were not antagonistic.

Aspects of Elaine's relationship with her father were also worked through in the group in ways which were different from what had occurred and what continued to occur in individual therapy. Two men in the group evoked transference responses that helped Elaine become aware of how she attempted to separate the sexually seductive aspect of her relationship with her father from the protective aspect. To Elaine, Ralph was the seductive, sexual father-brother. Ralph brought into the interaction complementary transferences. He had had a very strong sexual feeling about his attractive, seductive older sister. In the group, Ralph and Elaine were able to analyze and work through the meanings of their intense involvement with each other.

Simultaneously, with transference distortions centered on Ralph, Elaine reacted to George, an older man in the group, as a good protective father. Here again they were able to work through the respective meanings of their transference distortions because of shared meanings. George was very uncomfortable with uncertainties. He saw himself as someone who was good at fixing things. When Elaine came to the group with complaints about her marriage, her professors, and even her landlord, George knew how to fix it. While she had basked in his help, she and the group began to deal with the meaning of such help for each of them.

In the group, the therapist has the opportunity to see the combination of accurate perceptions and transference distortions in the interactions between patients. The therapist and the patient see how reciprocal and complementary transferences are dealt with. As Ralph was seductive with women, George was paternal and protective. Elaine could perceive the reality of each person, but in generalizing one aspect of them as the total person, she was forced to confront her transference distortions.

When patients reexperience family interactions in the therapy group, it is a function of a complex interaction of transferences and induced reactions, parallel to the complementary countertransferences described by Heinrich Racker (1972). In this way, the core of each person's neurotic interaction is brought into the group. The addition of group therapy helped Elaine to get beyond the childhood experiences that had affected all of her relationships. The process of working through in combined analytic therapy made it possible for her to evaluate and relate more realistically to those in her world of the present. She was able to achieve a more integrated sense of herself, to separate more effectively from her parents, and to build a new relationship with her husband.

The entrance of a new member to the group provided an example of the ways in which treatment needs can intersect and the therapy process be amplified. Ruth, a petite, pert redhead came into the group after three-and-a-half years of individual therapy. She was a successful business executive and initially had expressed some resistance to group therapy. But the realistic problems of time and job pressures were screens for the more important fears of changing the dyadic relationship. An only child, Ruth had found a good mother in her maternal aunt. In her fantasy, she and her Aunt Rose were alike. With her aunt as an idealized mother, she was able to intensify her feelings of special closeness with her father. Aunt Rose was unmarried and lived alone, and Ruth felt preferred by her over all others. She enjoyed the present status of things, and, as she said, she was always happy being "an only child."

Ruth saw the group as an interference in her relationship with her therapist. In the group, Ruth began to be aware of her terror of competition. She never ventured into situations where she could not win, and the prospect of entering group threatened her sense of being special. She had agreed to enter the group understanding its value, but had expressed her resistance by stating it was only because the therapist "thought it would be good for her." For Ruth, it was an intellectual experiment. The group was initially put off by her, but soon came to appreciate her quick perceptions and her sense of humor. She joked about her "quirks" and minimized her problems. She became a good buddy to the men and a wise older sister to the women.

Meanwhile, in her individual sessions, Ruth began to express her fears that these roles would wear thin and that she would begin to act as she usually did—seductive with the men, and competitive with the women. Then she would lose whatever good feeling she had managed to establish, and the therapist would begin to hate her. Ruth also expressed an awareness of her intense competitive feelings, but was reluctant to give them up. She felt that she always could use these feelings to her advantage—she won most competitions—and she was very jealous of the success she had achieved in the business world. To lose her success, or to lose those things she felt the success was based on—that is, both her seductiveness and her sharp competitiveness—was very frightening to her.

The therapist chose to make a transference interpretation rather than reassure Ruth at that point. She was able to help Ruth understand that she was reacting to her fantasy of the reaction in the group, that what she had found as a child was being reformed here. The parallels to her family situation were renewed and the meanings of the complex relationships between her parents and her aunt were seen in a new light.

The feedback from the group and the expansion of the therapeutic field that came with the partial disruption of the dyadic relationship became very important in Ruth's treatment. As Ruth was more open with the group, they gave clearer responses to her. They noted that though she spoke to them, she always seemed to watch for the therapist's response to her. They were also quick to point out how she disavowed her own nonverbal seductive behavior. She was able to listen to the group with more comfort as she accepted her need to be there for more than just the "experience." At the same time, Ruth was increasingly successful in her business career and could begin to reexamine her fears that the success was not real. She felt that it had not really been based on her abilities, but that she had seduced others into voting for her promotions.

The entrance of a new member to the group can amplify the treatment process as the needs of several group members intersect. Elaine was particularly responsive to Ruth's feelings about her seductiveness and her underlying poor self-esteem, and envied what she felt was Ruth's less troublesome seductive relationship with her father and her apparent lack of fear. As the two women were able to share and help each other work through the cost of that special daughter-father seductive relationship, old issues were clarified for them. But when Jane came into the group, Ruth's concern about a special position reemerged. She saw Jane as a younger version of herself, an attractive, successful woman, and felt that there should not be two of them in the same group. She was convinced that this was the therapist's secret message to her that she would have to go. Jane felt burdened by this assignment, and the other women were enraged. The men in the group also responded with anger at Ruth's view of her special position in the group.

The therapist was surprised by the intensity of Ruth's reaction to Jane. She had anticipated an expression of competitiveness, but had not expected it to take this form. The countertransference issues revolved around the feelings evoked in the therapist by Ruth's enjoyment of her feeling of being special. Ruth could create an aura in the individual session of a "specialness" that somehow became engaging for the therapist without her being aware of it. Thus the therapist was surprised when Ruth saw Jane's arrival as a signal that she would be abandoned. It had not occurred to the therapist that Ruth would feel so uncertain and precarious in her relationship to the therapist. As the therapist became aware of her counter-transference reactions, she was then able to work with Ruth around these issues.

During the period when all this was happening, Elaine had a dream that seemed to deal with the feelings of deprivation both she and Ruth experienced in relation to the therapist. She said, "I dreamed last night I was in a laundromat. All the machines are filled up. My friend is using five of the machines. I went to use them. There was one broken one, and someone had four others." She added, "I know laundry dreams have to do with therapy. I had a sense recently of wanting more therapy time but not having the time or money to do that. The one machine who's broken is like Ruth, who keeps talking about leaving the group. I'm going to miss her." The dream expressed the fears of both women that unless they had the special connection to the therapist—either symbiotic attachment or star role—they could not survive. These blocks to real autonomy and individuation surfaced and were clarified in the group. They were more accessible and could be worked through by both women.

Combined analytic therapy allows for the reworking of insights and previously achieved understandings that have not yet been changed into meaningful and established behavioral changes. The group has the possibility of providing the opportunity for a reworking—both individually and in its interactions—of insights that have been achieved earlier. In the case of Elaine, we see how old issues reemerged and were reworked yet again in the group situation. The impact of the feedback, as well as the shared experiences and emotional exchanges that are possible in a group, allow for a fuller working through not only of emotionally consistent insight, but also of appropriate behaviors. Behaviors in the group change as they are monitored by fellow group members and they have a chance to reexplore the meaning of their own and each other's behaviors in the group interactions. The working-through process in the group is particularly valuable because it not only develops insight, but also provides ways to learn new behaviors. The group supplies encouragement and reinforcement as well as a variety of experiences that cannot take place in the exclusivity of the individual therapy relationship.

CHAPTER 5

Dreams in the Working-Through Process

THROUGHOUT recorded history, dreams have been unique in man's total experience. The particular understandings of what a dream is, where it comes from, and its relationship to the dreamer have varied. Each culture has understood the dream in the context of the culture's total belief system and its social structure. But quite consistent throughout is the conviction that the dream is a unique communication, that special knowledge and more lucid understanding is encased in the dream.

Some History about Attitudes toward Dreams

The ancients' recognition of the mystery of the dream was evidenced in their attributing the dream to external forces. In the Old Testament, it was believed that dreams came from

God and could be interpreted only by those close to Him. Joseph was empowered to predict the future from the dreams of Pharoah, and the Homeric poets never spoke of "having a dream" but of "seeing one" (Bergmann 1966, 356). Martin Bergmann traces the gradual acceptance of dreams as intrapsychic phenomena. He finds isolated instances in the Hebrew tradition where the attempt is made to consider the dream not as a divine message, but as an intrapsychic event. Bergmann buttresses his argument by quoting from Jeremiah, "Neither harken to your dreams, which ye caused to be dreamed," and from the Talmud, "A man is shown [in a dream] from the thoughts in his own heart."

In Sophocles' *Oedipus*, Jocasta makes no attempt to invoke supernatural forces to explain the unacceptable incestuous wishes in dreams: "But fear not though touching wedlock with thy mother. Many men ere now have so fared in dreams also; but he to whom these things are as naught bears his life most easily."

The capacity for man not only to know the unacceptable and the frightening, but to express it symbolically adds another important dimension to the wonderment of dreams. Rollo May expresses it most articulately (Caligor and May 1968, 4): ". . . that dreaming has some connection with man's distinctive capacity for transcendence, i.e., his capacity to break through the immediate objective limits of existence and bring together into one dramatic union diverse dimensions of experience." May goes on to discuss the translogical quality of dreams and to refer to the work of Jung and Fromm as explications. Both argued that dreams reveal not only greater error and evil but also greater wisdom and ethical sensitivity. Moreover, both of these authors had an appreciation of the ability in dreams to synbolize with a poetry and lucidity usually not available in the conscious life of the dreamer.

Dreams in the Working-Through Process

Freud's work, beginning with dreams and proceeding to the development of psychoanalysis, laid the groundwork for our contemporary use of dreams in combined therapy (S.E. 1953).

First, Freud taught us to understand the elaborate "dream work," decoding the manifest dream when the dreamer has disguised its latent meaning and unacceptable expressions or wishes through displacement and condensation. But further, Freud appreciated and discussed the remarkable symbolization in dreams, a capacity less emphasized in traditional psychoanalytic writings where the focus was on associations to the dream as a pathway to the past. "Symbolism is perhaps the most remarkable chapter of the theory of dreams. In the first place, since symbols are stable translations, they realize to some extent the ideal of the ancient as well as of the popular interpretation of dreams, from which without technique, we had departed unduly. They allow us in certain circumstances to interpret a dream without questioning the dreamer." (S.E. 1961, 151) It is this aspect of dreams that makes the dream so potent a communication in group therapy. For many people, the symbols in their dreams are more articulate in expressing their essence than they can even approximate in the dialogue of their waking life.

Dreams in the Individual Phase of Combined Analytic Treatment

During the first phase of combined therapy, the individual treatment phase, the therapist's particular techniques in working with dreams become established. Primary for these therapists is the experiencing of the dream—the communication the dream brings about the less conscious aspects of the patient's present. In the dream perceptions of the patient and his relationship to others are expressed which are only beginning to come into consciousness. The dream also provides important clarification of the patient's defensive structure and valuable links to past memories.

Gradually, questions that the therapist would raise are answered without their being asked. The persons and places in the dream are identified and associated to. The sense experiences and the moods felt are frequently commented on. If the day's happenings which set off the dream have not been talked about prior to the recounting of the dream, they are reviewed at that point in the session.

The therapist's interventions about those aspects of the dream that reflect what is going on in the particular session and in the treatment process generally educate the patient to respond to transference issues. The dream dependably reveals transference reactions, both positive and negative. Many patients can acknowledge these reactions more easily when they are represented in the dream. Dreams of being invited into the therapist's home, or finding comfort in the presence of a companion with some link to the therapist, make it possible for some patients to talk of tender, yearning, or loving feelings which ordinarily are awkward for them to get to. Dreams of reluctant visits to the dentist, or of experiences with a neglectful building superintendent, provide entree for expressions of some of the more negative feelings toward therapy such as anger, or disdain, or of being exploited or demeaned. For many patients it is more possible to talk of these feelings after they have been introduced through the dream.

By the time a patient comes into group, he or she has learned to work collaboratively with the therapist, to understand dreams by giving associations, to attend to strong feelings or involvements associated with part of the dream, and to go after associations to elements or symbols not immediately fathomed.

The patient has learned that the therapist will respond differently to dreams at different times, encouraging associations to elements in some instances, deciphering symbols in others, and at times picking up on obvious transference reactions. The therapist might note that the dream reflects the feeling the patient has of making a step forward through "moving into the driver's seat," or trying a new solution ("stepping out of the icy street instead of standing immobilized").

As our patients have become involved in their analytic treatments, they more and more look to dreams to clarify feelings and thoughts that have been conflicting and confusing. They come first to *owning* their dreams—that is, experiencing the connections between their dreams and their waking life. Later they come to depend on the dreams for the reflection of their most authentic experiences. People and places occurring in dreams frequently represent memories that have been neglected for many years. The dream images provide links to related conflicts occurring in the present.

Dreams at Transition into Group

At the point where group is introduced to the treatment, dreams frequently reflect the anxieties stirred up in anticipation of the move into the group. As noted in chapter 3, these dreams can be general anxiety dreams. Kohut (1977, 140) discussed this kind of symbolization in dreams and its reflection of a generalized anxiety. Kohut suggested that the more vulnerable patient is very likely to have dreams which are an attempt to deal with the dreaded danger of dissolution of the self by symbolizing fears with nameable visual imagery. Dreams of the loss of teeth or hair or of bugs swarming all over fall into this category.

At other times the dreams are simple and direct reflections of the ambivalence the patient is experiencing about going into group. An example is the woman who reported dreaming that she was in a bus, realized she didn't like it, and just got off and went into her own car. This woman was struggling hard to accept being part of the "busload," and was finding it very difficult to relinquish the more gratifying attunement that was possible in her dyadic treatment.

Another patient expressed ambivalence and anxiety about going into group in separate symbols. In one night she dreamed of a rocket going off, a cat hiding in a corner of her room, and a mouse lured into a plastic bag by the offer of food. This woman felt excited at the prospect of going into the group, but also felt frightened, inclined to pull back, and terrified by the feelings of mistrust and ambivalence that were surfacing in relation to her therapist.

The dream image can make a succinct statement about a person's inner state, expressing a complex set of feelings visually. The "bus" or Elaine's "suspension bridge" (Chapter 4) are examples of images that condense complex meanings and are slowly revealed in the patient's associations. Another example of this is Roger's dream. After his third group session, Roger came to his individual session saying he had been edgy since midweek. He couldn't really explain it:

"I was in a train, traveling very fast. There were different people, but I can't tell you who." In response to the therapist's questions, Roger said he was sitting like everyone else and feeling "not bad but a little uneasy." Associations led back to the group session. Roger had been feeling peripheral to the group. He felt he was not in control at all, that things were going too fast. It brought to mind his father's injunctions when he was a child, to be "careful," "not to get dirty," and "not to get into trouble." He realized he associated being out of control with doing something bad. He was reexperiencing the intense anxiety he had felt at such times since childhood.

Dreams in the Group

The approach to dreams in the group is a direct function of the therapist's orientation and attitudes as its members tend to reflect and thus amplify their previous experience with the same therapist's encouragement or discouragement of dreams, both conscious and unconscious.

In the group situation, the responses of both the dreamer and the other group members to the dream are a continuation of the analytic process from the individual session. When the dreamer's report of a dream does not spontaneously offer the elaboration that patients are accustomed to give about their own dreams, another group member may raise them—questions like "What happened today?" "Who was that person?" or "What were you feeling?"

When a patient brings a dream to the group, the therapist's first focus is on the dream as a communication from the dreamer to the group, including the therapist. A woman new to a group brought in the following dream in her third session there: "I was in a bathroom sitting on a toilet. The door was open. Bill [a man in the group who had responded warmly and protectively to her] said, 'Why don't you close the door?' I felt very grateful to him. It was as if I didn't realize that I had the choice."

Group members picked up that the new patient, tending to be compliant with the therapist, had not realized that she had felt obligated to "shit in public," that this was one meaning of being in the group. The therapist added that she understood, too, that the patient had not felt protected by her in the group and had welcomed the group members stepping in to give her the aid she needed.

When the dream is vivid, the group gets engaged and proceeds without intervention from the therapist. When Ted reported a dream in which Matt was doing a graceful but stylistically repetitive Virginia Reel, people smiled in immediate recognition of Matt's way of moving adroitly away from confronting some issues. After some animated group exchange about this, focusing on Matt and Ted's perceptiveness, the therapist wondered aloud about why Ted had dreamed this. The group then moved toward surfacing the subtle presence of a similar characterological strain in Ted.

Incorporating group members into the manifest content of a dream gives us another view of how group works in the total treatment process. The group session is part of the residue of the day, and may trigger the manifest content of the dream. Other group members act in a manner familiar and linked to past experience, but the current relationship with the other group members has the potential to be different. There is an opportunity for the adult ego to deal effectively with something the patient could not cope with at an earlier point in his life.

When there is no response to a dream, it is the therapist's task to understand how this relates to the group process and to the ambivalence of the dreamer. How far this is explored at the moment, or whether it is explored in the group at all, will

Dreams in the Working-Through Process

depend on the individual dynamics of the patient and the relationship of this to what is going on in the group at the moment.

Confronting the issue of non-response in the group is likely to heighten the patient's anxiety and defensiveness. If the group is usually responsive to the patient's needs and this particular situation is an exception, it might prove productive to press further to elicit a response. However, if the non-response is something that the patient characteristically evokes, it might be an error to raise the issue in the sensitive context of a dream.

In 1953, Eva Klein-Lipschutz made the observation that dreams reported in group were briefer. She attributed this to the confrontation of defenses in group therapy and the consequent openness and directness shown by group patients. This may be so, but there is another possible explanation of the same data. People quickly find out that a group tends to get impatient and resentful of long dream accounts because of the demand they place on the group's time. Thus, brief dreams, which communicate quickly and immediately, are more readily presented.

This tendency is further supported by the intuitive inclination of patients to bring to the individual session dreams that are likely to take more time; that is, dreams that are more ambiguous, that make the dreamer feel more vulnerable or hypersensitive, or dreams that are more obsessively defensive. In the individual session, the dream will get the time it needs and the understanding the dreamer requires with a fair guarantee of consideration to the patient's sensitivities. For example, the following dream was very deliberately brought to an individual session by a thirty-one-year-old woman. The content in the individual session prior to reporting the dream had to do

155

with thoughts of having a baby and the mounting desire in this direction, an account of more involved sexual experience, and a reference to a good conversation the patient had had with her father, with whom she had recently been establishing a more gratifying relationship. Recently they had been sharing some of their interests on the telephone. The following is the woman's dream.

"It was in my apartment. I walked into the bedroom. The window was wide open, curtains gently blowing in the wind. It was a very warm day. There was a child in the room, a three-year-old boy. I realized he must have come in the window. I got terrified for the child and his getting into the room through the window. He could have been hurt. I knew he belonged to me. I washed him and bathed him, and it felt so good. I remember him sleeping. I somehow found out who his parents were, and I returned him."

In this dream, the patient was symbolically reclaiming aspects of herself that she had begun to split off and dissociate from since she was three. There was great sensitivity, openness, and tenderness in her voice and manner, and it was important for her to share it in private in the individual session. This very vulnerability was central to her difficulty in building intimacy with men. It was too new, and she felt too vulnerable to bring this dream into the less predictable environment of the group. Perhaps at some future point she would be able to do this, but for the present the patient needed to experience and reconstruct the dream in her individual session. She recalled very early experiences, looked again at her defensive mechanisms for coping with these, and could link the past with the present.

Some earlier psychoanalytic group writers considered bringing a dream to the individual session instead of to the group to be resistance to the group process. But as we move toward

Dreams in the Working-Through Process

a more collaborative view of psychoanalytic treatment, with more respect for the patient's role in his own treatment, we better appreciate the patient's differential use of the two modalities.

As the patient becomes involved in group, transference reactions proliferate and the cast of characters in dreams more frequently includes group members. Elaine (chapter 4) included two of the men in her group in a dream to represent two aspects of her feelings towards her father. Ted expressed aspects of himself in a dream by using a group member who epitomized these characteristics. He had indirectly expressed his problems with procrastination by describing Matt and the Virginia Reel, and at another time, he dreamed, "John was kissing Meg in this public cafe. I tapped him on the shoulder and said, 'This is a public place, you know.' He didn't care. He just went on kissing her." John, a fairly impulsive young man, was comfortable with doing what he wanted to do. Ted's envy was related to his conflict between an inclination to be free and possibly exhibitionistic and a repressive code permitting none of this.

Whether the dream will be reported in the individual session or in the group is determined by the particular circumstances. If the patient is in a fairly non-resistant phase and is working productively with both the members of the group and the therapist, he or she is likely to bring the dream to whichever session follows its occurrence. It may then be reintroduced in the other modality. Bert, who was in the end phase of his treatment and close to resolving his central transference issues, brought a dream in to this individual session: His father needed to have the car fixed, and told him so on the phone. Bert said, "My father told me he trusted me to take care of whatever was needed. I didn't have to check with him at all." Bert was close to tears in the session, as he spoke openly of how much he valued the new closeness and trust that he was developing with his father. His dream expressed a deep inner experience and acceptance of this. In the next group session, Bert was reminded of the dream by another member's account of a painful encounter with his father, and Bert recounted his dream to the group.

At other times a dream will be introduced in group and some aspects will be attended to but others not, so it will be brought to the individual session for more exploration. It is the patient's decision whether the dream will be brought to the individual or the group. It is unwise for the therapist to urge the patient to bring a dream reported in the individual session into the group. If the patient is not motivated to tell the dream at that time, the reluctance will be apparent either in tone or in manner. The report of the dream will probably fall flat and interfere with the very goal that would have been achieved if the patient was ready to share it with the other group members.

When a patient does report a dream in group, there is valuable information available in addition to the content and quality of the dream. There is the dreamer's behavior while relating the dream, whom he or she looks at, body position, and body movements. The affect with which the patient relates the dream is another important part of the communication. Timing, either sensitive to the needs of others or oblivious to them, is also important in revealing something about the patient and predicting the group's response.

Patients determine much of how their dreams will be received in their handling of them, revealing much of their individual personality styles in the process. Some volunteer their own associations; others wait to be asked. Some will control the other group members' responses to their dreams, rejecting some, accepting others (including the therapist) in support of a position they hold on the nature of the dream.

Dreams in the Working-Through Process

Others will passively turn the dream over to the therapist and the group for analysis. The therapist's response will depend on an estimate of the group process and the therapeutic need of the dreamer at that moment.

People are particularly sensitive to the reactions of others to their dreams. Therapists' interventions attending to the reactions from the group can help the dreamer cope with narcissistic injury experienced from either being ignored or misunderstood. Both reactions are inevitable in group at least part of the time. The group process can result in a dream not being discussed. The individual's need to pursue his dream can be in conflict with the interest of the other group members. The therapist's judgment will determine whether note of this is made in the group or in the individual session.

The content of the individual session following the group will frequently touch on issues of the dream. If the patient does not refer to it or does not seem to recall the dream, the therapist may wonder at the omission. There may be a question about how the patient felt at the group's reaction to the dream. This is important to the process as it helps to avoid future blocking in recalling dreams, which can occur when they are not adequately heard in therapy.

In a group that has been working together, a dream of one group member evokes associations from others to symbolic expressions of their own. This more direct and immediate communication of the dream occurs when people in the group are feeling more open and undefensive. The familiarity with each other and individual styles of presentation seems to remove barriers from responding directly to the dream. For example, a man reported this dream in a group: "I was heading through a tunnel. I saw a light. I was going this way. [And he pointed.] Some people on horseback were heading the other way. [Again he indicated with his hands the opposing direction.] A heavy material covered the person and the horse. The people were all covered up."

The dreamer felt that the dream had to do with individual sessions and group sessions sometimes seeming to go in opposite directions. He went into detail about the heaviness of the material that was covering the person and the horse; it was like denim. Gail, a woman in the group, recognized the covering up of the figures as a kind of encasing of defensiveness that she knew and knew the dreamer knew. The difference was that the image in her dreams was of encasement in a transparent, plastic, equally confining material, but material you could see through. Adam, a man in the group, associated to a dream he had discussed in individual treatment but had not brought into group until then. He said, "The same way you saw the light and pulled back I once had a dream that I was having a baby through my mouth, and then the baby went back down. It was the same feeling that I was coming out, this new person, and then sliding back at moments." Adam was able to reveal to the group a very personal and disturbing feeling at this moment in response to the dream he had just heard. Until then, the experiences in his own dreams had seemed too personal, too uncomfortable to articulate in the group.

Sometimes in a group accustomed to working with dreams, the quality of the dreamer's distance from the dream makes it easier to communicate hurt feelings or other embarrassing experiences to the therapist or to the group members. "I was standing in line in your home [the patient pointed to the therapist for emphasis] for chicken dinner. I was not sure why it was taking so long to get to me." This very shy woman had been unable to speak in group about her hurt feelings or the anxious concern she felt when she was unable to express herself unless the therapist helped her. Through this dream she was able to tell her fellow group members an embarrassing piece of information about herself and to elicit their help in articulating it and dealing more directly with it.

In another instance, a young man reported the following dream. He had gone to the airport to meet his mother. His girl friend came with him. In the process he somehow lost or misplaced his car. This patient disliked his inclination to see the many connections between his mother and his girl friend, but felt he needed to talk about it in group; he then used the dream to introduce the subject.

Dreams help surface subtleties of transference issues. Many patients are more likely to acknowledge both positive and negative transference reactions when they are represented in the dream. "A Nazi woman was commandant of a group. She snipped my lip with scissors whenever I spoke up and had differences with her." The young woman patient hesitantly reported the dream in the group, some challenge in her voice. She was aware of fears and involved feelings toward the therapist and the transferential intensity of them. But the dream was a vehicle that permitted her to bring up the issue in group, which she had not been able to do until then. Similarly, a man reported, "I was dancing with Ellen [the therapist]. She was showing me some new steps, and I could do them. It was great."

The use of dreams in working through in combined therapy is a complex process. An account of one patient's experience will give the reader a sense of the process: May came to her individual session with a dream that followed a group session that stirred her awareness of the considerable socioeconomic differences among the members in the group.

"I dreamed that I was part Korean. In the dream, for the first time, it dawned on me that my father is part Korean. In my dream, his eyes got slantier. Then I was at a big party in a cafeteria-type place. Neal, a guy who used to be my agent, was being held up. He was so white, and his eyes were closed. I had ordered my lunch. They brought me appetizer, a piece of fish. Brenda [an older executive in the patient's firm] walked by smiling, saying, 'It was okay you ordered that.' It was okay even though it was expensive and she was paying for it."

The first segment of the dream about Koreans expressed May's subtle feelings of inferiority. May's associations to Koreans reflected her view of them as helpless and ineffective, which she also saw as true of her father. The discussion of socioeconomic differences in the group had made her aware of these shaky feelings, feelings she tried to push away. May identified with her father's passivity and helplessness. She also expressed this in her image of her former agent white with fright and with his eyes closed. Father had not seemed to see anything that was going on. The party in the cafeteria related to the group and May's conflict between her great need for nurturing and acceptance, her fear of asking for too much and being rejected, and her fear of evoking anger in the therapist or in the group.

May's ambivalence to the therapist and the group is expressed in the multiple meanings of "being held up." The first association was to being held up, accosted. But she wasn't so sure that was what was happening, maybe it was "held back," or even "propped up." May connected these associations with ambivalent feelings she had had in the group and sometimes in individual sessions. She appreciated the support of the therapy but feared exploitation by it.

In her individual session, May talked of her envy of two other women in the group and the relationship they had with the therapist, their comfort and sureness in it, and their ability to interact so much more freely than she did.

May also told her next dream in the individual session: "Brenda was sitting across from me. There was eye contact. I was excited about talking to her. I was waiting for her to ask about my business. She looked kind of like you. She smiled but was not so interested. She got up to put lipstick on. It was disappointing. I thought finally I'd have had something to talk to her about that would interest her, but I hadn't."

May felt that she couldn't compete for the therapist, that she wasn't interesting enough and wasn't valued enough, just as she couldn't compete with her siblings for mother or for father. She went on to recall yet again the feelings of being unloved, unwanted, and a burden. She was aware that in the dream Brenda represented the therapist and the ambivalent feelings May felt toward her.

At the next group session, May brought in a dream about the group. She and another woman both wanted the floor. As usual, May withdrew, but Penny, another group member, noted the withdrawal and helped her to get the attention she needed. May felt unsure that the attention would last. The group responded to May's dream with awareness of her hesitancy toward taking group time for herself and her readiness to surrender a position of attention when she had one. Group members told May they saw her inability to compete for the attention of the therapist or the group. May was then able to proceed to sharing more of her feelings of shakiness and insecurity. She described the family scene she reexperienced in the group and expressed her wish to have the courage to make it different.

The Dream as a Deliberate Communication to the Group

Patients use their dreams to bring to the group an inner experience that is not apparent unless articulated. This dream was first brought to an individual session: "I was going to a resort located at the top of a mountain. I was in an elevator in the middle of the mountain. It was going up and up, through the middle, until I finally got to the top, and it was a resort under construction—bulldozed land, uncovered earth where they were beginning to build."

The patient who had this dream was advanced in the treatment process. The dream recapitulated the history of her treatment. It represented her coming up out of a depression, becoming energized, and pushing through to light and sun and air. The dream communicated both the elation at getting there and the arduousness of the process, the effort it had taken. There was awareness that there was hard work still to be done.

The patient brought this dream in, though, as a good dream, one she enjoyed talking about, and associated in the session to a real past experience of ascending by elevator through a mountain to the Wolf's Nest in Germany. She had the same feeling of exhilaration and excitement now about coming to a place where she really felt free of much of the past constriction and ready to start constructing a life that was going to be different. The uncovered earth in her dream expressed the newness, the rawness, and the unfinished quality of her task. The description of the land spelled out the resistances that persisted. "Bulldozed" had connections with the patient's mistrust, her feeling of being assaulted by interpretations despite their apparent utility. The "uncovered" aspect of the earth symbolized her defenseless feeling as she became more aware of what she did.

This dream occurred right before the individual session and was brought there, but the patient later brought it into the group. The dream expressed where she felt she was right then better than any description she could offer, and it communicated her feelings to the group.

Dream Work in the Group as a Source of Self-Esteem

In group work with dreams, both the presenter and the other group members get an unusual opportunity to experience positive feelings about themselves. The dreamer gets the chance to experience the others' wonderment at his precise and lucid images. There is frequently a hushed moment after a dream is told, simply because it communicates so completely there is no need for words. A man who had described feeling bad about mistreatment in a business deal described this odd dream: He was "fucking" a man, then realizes that, "I was being fucked over!" A woman described disgust at her dream: "I walked into the bathroom and stepped into his [her husband's] shit." Or another woman who was coming out of a depressed period who told of a dream of having forgotten to water her plants and suddenly remembering watering them, and finding to her tremendous relief that they were able to come alive; in fact, a flower appeared.

There is also an opportunity for the respondents to the dream to provide reactions and resonances for it that are particularly empathic, sometimes more so than either the therapist or other group members. It provides another corrective to the idealization of the therapist and an improvement in self-esteem in relation to peers.

In summary, throughout the combined analytic therapy experience dreams deepen the level of communication in the total treatment process, but particularly in the group, where dreams provide immediacy and vividness in relation to each other's inner experiences.

CHAPTER 6

The Termination Process

The Case of Blanche

Seven minutes before the end of the group session, during a moment of silence, Blanche said, "I have to announce something. I'm going to be leaving group." Anticipating a rebuke for bringing this up at the end of the session, Blanche added, "I know there's no time to talk about it now, but I didn't want another week to go by without letting everybody know."

Blanche then turned to the therapist and asked if it was necessary to come in for an individual session. (For two years her regular therapy had been only in group. The rare individual sessions were initiated at her request.) When asked what her preference was about having an individual session, Blanche said that she would rather not have one, but was willing to accept the therapist's recommendation. The therapist decided to follow Blanche's inclination, with the understanding that she take responsibility for using group time to examine her decision. Blanche was better at taking time for herself than she used to be, but was still inclined to let others' needs take precedence. Four more sessions were agreed on.

In the last few moments of the session, a number of group members expressed their regret about losing Blanche's participation in the group. As the group member who had been in it the longest, Blanche brought that experience to her natural perceptiveness and intelligence. She regularly made valuable contributions to the group process. Blanche was clear about her decision to leave; it was time—she had been in the group for five years. The two newest members in the group were startled at the length of her membership. Blanche said that she was going to explain it more next week, but that she had been seriously depressed most of her life and had stayed on in the group for the last year to be sure that she was really past her depression. As the group concluded, the second oldest member murmured that Blanche's decision made him realize that he had just been coasting along and was not really dealing with ending himself. The therapist was aware of the fact that Blanche's decision was not really a surprise; she had been anticipating it.

About ten minutes into the following group session there was a pause. The therapist looked at Blanche, and Blanche responded to her look with, "Yes, I wanted to talk about it. I've decided that the time has come for me to leave." The two newest members were particularly interested in how Blanche knew she was really ready. Neither the woman, in the group for six months, nor the man, who had been in it only three weeks, had a sure sense of how group was really going to make a difference for them. They were eager to learn from Blanche.

Blanche said, "My depression is not a problem any more, but it was a problem for a long time." She went on to say that she had stayed in the group, attending even though she really wanted the time for other things, because the group was a security blanket. She had been afraid to let go of it. It was hard for her to believe that her depression was really gone. Blanche explained that she had been depressed since she was fourteen years old, and she had thought she would never change.

The new members asked Blanche to tell them something of how her depression had started. Blanche spoke quietly, without apparent anger or shame, of the constant fighting in her home between her alcoholic father, who worked as an unskilled laborer, and her mother, who "just wasn't there mentally." As a young child, she realized it was truly hopeless to expect either one of them to understand her. She had found her only escape in books, reading voraciously. Blanche said that reading had deepened her sadness, as she realized the vast distance between her world and the larger world she was discovering in books.

When asked what she meant by "depression," Blanche replied, "It's when you lie on the sofa with a cup of tea for hours and you don't do anything, even though there's a lot to do."

The six group members were engaged by Blanche's account. The therapist was aware of a very different tone as Blanche told her history and "defined" her depression. The past had been put in place and the perspective came from an observing ego and a less critical, more accepting sense of self.

As she observed the group, the therapist realized that everyone present had had some struggles with depression. She commented that every person there knew, from their own experience, something of what Blanche was talking about.

The therapist watched Matthew, the new member in the group, as she made the observation about the ubiquitousness of depression. Initially, he had told the group he was only in it to learn about himself and others to further his career. She thought Matthew might take defensive exception to her generalization. Instead, he was sober and silently contemplative. The therapist knew that he had serious, debilitating bouts of depression, which had been his primary impetus for coming into treatment.

Nan, the newest woman in the group, asked Blanche if she could tell them what had changed for her. Blanche said it was simple, in a way. She had realized, in group and in individual therapy, that she had to move out into the world and stop withdrawing from it. It was simple to say this now, but it was not simple doing it; it had taken years. She had had no friends, no career, and little connection with anything outside her house. She said that before she returned to school, she was a "housewife who couldn't keep house." She could hardly believe it, but this had all really changed for her, certainly not all at once, but gradually. She had always tended to her children, but now she really had a good time with them. She had a boyfriend she could really enjoy. (Blanche had been widowed with very young children, and after some time with no relationships, had had a series of disappointing ones which had contributed further to her feeling of hopelessness.)

Blanche told the group that she was going to miss them, particularly the members she had known for years, but that that was not a reason to stay. The therapist asked Blanche what her sense was of people's feelings about her. She was silent for a moment and then answered, "I know that people think better of me than I expect them to. I've learned that."

Blanche started her last session by telling how terribly sad she was feeling; it was something like the feeling she had when people close to her died, an awful loss. Nonetheless, she knew that she should move on.

Blanche chose to "go around" in her farewells to the group, giving a personal goodbye to each group member, and speaking of the changes she had seen in each and offering insightful suggestions for their continued therapy. For example, to a man who had never truly nurtured another human being, she suggested that he start with a plant and take care of it; it would be easier than a pet. He smiled shyly at Blanche's recognition of his readiness to care for someone or something and his inexperience with it.

The Decision to Terminate Therapy

The decision to terminate treatment is arrived at gradually, reflecting movement on different levels of understanding, intrapsychic organization, and behavior. Patients will have an understanding of their difficulties and how they developed in terms of their own history. Persistent transference distortions will have been identified, interpreted, and modified. They have made changes in their defensive system and are attuned to when and where they become defensively vulnerable. There have been behavioral changes and they have come to terms with the reality of their lives. All these gains mark increasing degrees of awareness. Although there is always more one can learn and experience, at some point both patient and therapist agree that they have arrived at the place where the increments of gains do not warrant continuing therapy. The self-awareness and ability to analyze their behavior that has been developed in the course of therapy hopefully will continue after they have left treatment. The less rational issues of dependency, gratifications of the relationship, and problems with separation in general are part of the termination phase of therapy.

Decisions for termination are best described in terms of the ongoing therapeutic process rather than in terms of cure. When psychoanalysis treated symptoms only, the question of when to terminate was simpler. If the analysis was successful, it ended when the symptoms disappeared. As analysis became the analysis of character, the question of at what point and in what manner to terminate became acute, and continues to be a problem (Bergmann 1966). Although termination is not widely written about, a recent review of the literature suggests that the process of termination itself provides therapeutic gains and is of analytic significance (Firestein 1978).

Termination is an important part of the continuing developmental model. The patient with a more realistic and strengthened sense of self, possessing an increased awareness of the genetic origins and meanings of his behavior, is able to separate from the therapist, ready to go on alone with a more satisfactory way of perceiving and interacting with the world.

The process of leaving without feeling that you have to destroy the loved object or risk being destroyed is an important developmental step. Separation that allows for continuity in terms of inner experiences is an important part of the analytic process. Some patients may experience this in the way that Elaine (chapter 4) did when she commented, "I don't need you in the same way any more. I can use your voice. It's like mine now; I can say things to myself now."

Therapists must also be aware of their own reluctance, at times, to deal with the process of termination. The gratifications they receive from working with particular patients may make it difficult to end the therapy at the point where those patients are still providing these narcissistic reinforcements. Therapists may also find it difficult to end therapy because of their own unrealistic expectations and goals for therapy. Both patients and therapists have to recognize the limitations of therapy. They must deal with their shared and differing experiences of loss that comes with the ending of the therapy relationship (Dewald 1982).

The reasons for and effects of termination are more importantly related to the goals of therapy as defined by the patient and the therapist than to some abstract and objective definition of cure (Gedo 1981). This becomes more important when we change our goals for therapy, when the work focuses less on cure or change related to symptom removal. We are more concerned with the analysis of character and changes that occur in terms of the patient's intrapsychic reality and interpersonal relationships. Thus, cure is not really a relevant concept, and the process of change is one that involves a larger time frame. Both patient and therapist may make decisions about termination without assuming that the process of change initiated in the therapy will end.

The Termination of Individual Therapy

Most patients in combined analytic therapy end individual treatment first and then continue in group alone. This final phase may vary from a few months to a few years and provides an extended opportunity for working through issues of separation and individuation, loss, and the achievement of autonomy.

The loss patients feel when individual therapy ends is real, even if termination is planned and carefully worked through. The intimacy and intensity of individual therapy provided a very special relationship. One consistent person has focused on the patient's needs, history, and current concerns. Even after the transference distortions have been resolved, there remains the reality of losing a unique relationship.

For patients in combined analytic therapy the phase of group alone provides an opportunity to work toward increasing autonomy while maintaining some connection to the therapist. They experience the loss of their special therapeutic relationship in ways that are reminiscent of the *rapprochement* phase described by Margaret Mahler (et al 1975). In the weekly group session they are then able to reaffirm for themselves that the therapist is still there.

When individual therapy ends and the patient is only in the group, there may be a greater use of the group, as though to make up for the loss of individual sessions. The patient's need for the group, and the greater dependence on peers, again parallels normal developmental sequences. There is a diminished importance of the authority figure and a greater reliance on peers for self-definition and support. Receiving help from peers makes both the giver and the receiver feel stronger.

Some patients may regress temporarily in the group when the individual therapy ends. When Irene terminated her individual therapy, she was seen again by the group as the "helpless little girl" she had been when she started group, crying constantly whenever she talked. As Irene and the group analyzed this behavior, she was able to make important connections. The end of her individual therapy sessions had evoked the feelings of loss and deep sense of loneliness that had first brought her into therapy. With the termination of individual sessions, regression had occurred. However as evidence of the working-through process the depth and the duration were shortened. As the patient gains the understanding to implement behavioral changes, there is an increased capacity to regain balance by confronting repetition.

The Importance of Planning Terminations in Group

When the patient feels that the goals set have been achieved, termination is planned. At least a month, often longer, is needed fully to explore and complete the process.

When a group member leaves as part of a planned termination, the process of ending the therapeutic relationship is productive for all the group members. They can associate to not only their hopes for themselves, but also to other experiences of separation and loss, such as times in their lives when the family circle was broken. One patient, Greg, recalled feelings he had when his older sister married and left the family. Ezra recalled mixed feelings of loneliness and triumph when his older brother left for college, saying that he had "lost an ally in family battles, but at least I finally had the whole room for myself."

Group members are often ambivalent when one person announces leaving the group. Feelings of hope for future change and pleasure in mutual growth are usually shared, but at the same time, feelings of disappointment are expressed. This is another step in the "optimal disillusionment of therapy" (Gedo 1979) in which no one emerges "perfect."

The issues of competition and envy, sibling rivalry, and ambivalence frequently emerge in the group at this time. A group member's "graduation" often draws comments in terms of how long the departing member had been in the group, when he or she started therapy, who was there before, and so forth, leading to a review of group history. Each group member must now confront his or her own ambivalence about remaining in therapy and the wish to leave. Group members must also deal with their feelings of loss and may speculate about what the group will be like without the departing member. Separation-individuation issues are reawakened in new ways. In some instances, a group member may respond to another member's announcement of termination plans with a sense of personal hurt: "How could you leave me?"

Sometimes the loss of a departing member is expressed in anger toward the therapist. Cathy exploded in anger at the therapist when Marjorie announced that she was planning to leave the group. Cathy stormed, "How can you look so pleased? Don't you care about her at all? After all these years, you don't look like you'll even miss her." The group was startled by Cathy's anger. Although each was aware of some feelings of ambivalence, the intensity of Cathy's rage somehow clouded the group's shared feelings of pride in Marjorie's growth. After a while, Vera expressed her empathy with Cathy's anger at the therapist. As the group worked with both women to explore their shared feelings, each made a connection to an early history of loss. Both Cathy and Vera had lost a parent as very young children.

In the context of Cathy and Vera's history, their anger at the therapist for her apparent lack of feeling for the departing member became understandable. The therapist suggested that the anger was related to what each had experienced as a small child facing the bewilderment of "How could he leave me? Didn't he care about me?" The therapist helped the two women deal with their anxiety at the loss of a group member, but more particularly, helped them deal with their feelings of danger and abandonment when the therapist seemed to be pleased with the separation. Because their early feelings of abandonment were revived by the prospect of Marjorie's departure, the therapist's calm acceptance was experienced as a break in empathy with their feelings. The acknowledgment of these feeling and the genetic interpretation were reparative.

In a well-planned termination, group members rework issues of separation and loss in a variety of ways. When Anthony announced that he would be leaving the group, there was an almost uniform expression of pleasure for him from the members, though they felt regret for themselves. There was a recognition on the part of several that they "knew it was coming."

Anthony had been an active and highly interactive group member. He had made significant gains in his five years of therapy and had been sharing with the group the pleasures he was experiencing in his "new life." His marriage had been revitalized, and he had made important strides in his career.

As the group worked with these positive feelings about Anthony's termination, others emerged. Competition and rivalry with Anthony were expressed. Ezra, who had been in the group almost as long as Anthony, was upset that he felt "nowhere near being ready to leave." He wondered if Anthony was better than he had been to start with or whether the therapist had really "given him more," as Ezra had always suspected. Sarah, who had come into the group with Anthony, felt envy and rivalry, even though she was planning to leave the group herself in a few months.

In Anthony's final session, having had several weeks to deal with the varied and often ambivalent responses to his departure, the group members expressed individually what he had meant to them. They discussed how they felt they had recognized his need to leave. Walter spoke of how important it was that he and Anthony came from the same part of the country and were able to share local language and events of childhood. It was a great help to Walter in feeling at home in the group. Ruefully, Walter said he still needed to deal with his fears of competition with other men; Anthony could have helped him with this, but he could not ask him to stay for that reason. Tom, whose problems with expressing anger had been his major concern in the group, was able to tell Anthony that observing his acceptance of his own anger had been very helpful to him. Like Walter, Tom regretted not being able to have more of Anthony's help. Sue told Anthony how his sensitivity to her feelings had been helpful to her. In the group she became able to face the impact and meaning of the incestuous feelings in her family. Two other women commented that Anthony's ability to commit himself to a long-term relationship and work out the problems in his marriage had been helpful to them. They became able to recognize their own unreasonable demands on their partners and see how destructive these had been.

As the group members spoke, the therapist acknowledged her own ambivalent feelings to herself. There was pleasure in seeing the results of the work she and Anthony had done: there were significant changes in his feelings, his view of himself, and in his behavior. Many of the goals Anthony had set for himself when he began therapy had been reached. At the same time, the therapist was aware of her sense of loss. Anthony had been a very important group member and, like the patients, she wondered what the group would be like without him.

So the loss of a valued member was experienced on a number of different levels. The group members, while acknowledging what they had received or still could receive from Anthony's participation in the group, were able to separate his needs from theirs. They were able to accept his need to leave and were ready to deal with their sense of loss and still let him go with good feelings for him and for themselves.

Premature or Precipitous Terminations

Since the departure of any individual will change the group configuration, premature or precipitous terminations may have wide-ranging repercussions for the group. Therapists quickly learn when there are errors in placing a patient in a group. If the patient is not ready to be in the group either in terms of self-awareness or a less than fully developed working alliance with the therapist, there is a likelihood of abrupt termination. This is disruptive not only to the patient involved but also to the group and to the ongoing therapy process for six or seven other people. Confidence in the therapist and in the combined therapy process may be shaken. Nevertheless, at some time it occurs in every group. Then the work of the group must proceed, exploring and understanding the impact of the precipitous termination on the group as a whole and on each individual.

There are instances when one can agree that it is in the patient's best interests that the therapy terminate even though the work of the therapy has not been completed. For example, Vera left therapy when her husband was offered an important position in another city. It was a major step in his career, and Vera was able to explore the meaning of his request that she leave with him. Her ability to make a choice was important; it was not like her father's sudden death, this time she had a part in the plan. Not feeling helpless left Vera free to decide to return to therapy when she was settled in her new home.

The group was able to accept Vera's decision as right for her at this point in her life. It forced them to reconsider their own expectations for themselves. The fantasies of therapy as rebirth, the hopes that they would emerge as perfect were considered. When Vera talked in confident tones of working with another therapist when she moved, group members had to explore the transference distortions involved in feeling that their particular therapist was "the only one" who could understand or be helpful.

When a patient leaves the group precipitously, group members may also experience shock, disappointment with the therapist, and guilt. Bruce was seen early in the evolution of the

model of combined analytic treatment, before we fully understood the importance of narcissistic problems and the impact
of a group on such patients. We learned from cases like
Bruce's, and this led to the clarification of our understanding
of the problems of such narcissistic patients in a group.

Bruce had been in group for about six months when he
stormed out of a session vowing never to return. He had been
in therapy for about five years with another therapist and had
left it very disillusioned about therapy, disappointed in the
therapist, and angry with his wife, who had been instrumental
in his undertaking and then ending therapy. After a period of
two years, in response to his wife's urging, he entered therapy
with a different therapist. This immediately suggested constraints on the kind of working alliance that could be con-
structed, as the committment and motivation were not his own
but were made to placate his wife. In addition, Bruce was very
vulnerable to the slightest narcissistic injury. Any difference
was experienced as an assault and as rejection.

Negative transferences were explored in Bruce's individual
therapy. In it, Bruce continually made unfavorable compari-
sons of his present therapist to his previous one. He declared
that he needed unequivocal love and support, that a "good"
therapist would always agree with him and help him get whatever he wanted. After about a year in individual therapy, the
therapist suggested group. Bruce's fantasy was that the group
would assist him in convincing the therapist of the importance
of gratifying his wishes. In various ingratiating ways, he tried
to have the group members form an alliance with him to secure
what he wanted from the therapist.

When Bruce began to be late for group sessions, the others
questioned him about the meaning of this behavior. He said
that though it delayed his arrival he met his friends for a drink

after work because it was important, it made him "feel good." As the group tried to pursue the meaning of this with Bruce, he got furious, left, and refused to return. The group immediately felt guilty that they had hurt Bruce and had not been understanding or empathic. Each group member explored his own transference reactions to Bruce. Some, though shocked, could not help but admire his "daring and defiance." However, these feelings led to their anger at the therapist: Why had she placed Bruce in the group before he was ready?

The therapist acknowledged how upsetting Bruce's departure was for all of them. She also had to review for herself why she had chosen to add group to Bruce's individual therapy at this time. She had anticipated that Bruce might trigger negative feelings among group members that might be helpful to group interactions, which had tended to avoid negative feelings recently. She was aware of the fact that the addition of group to individual therapy creates additional stresses. The therapist is always involved in making choices, weighing possible gains against strains; there is no exact prediction possible for every choice. The therapist also had to explore her own countertransferences. Her feelings about what was happening in the group at that time, as well as her feelings about the work with Bruce in individual treatment, entered into her choice. The toll that narcissistic patients with paranoid defenses can take on the therapist conceivably underlies the numerous referrals of such patients to group. However, experience has taught us that such a move is frequently not helpful for the patient or for the group.

It may take a group several weeks to deal with the disruption of a precipitous termination. Although one does not plan such an experience, it can be used to advantage, as long as the therapist does not feel too apologetic about the referral mistake.

There are times, too, when the therapist will support a patient's wish to leave group while at the same time acknowledging that there still may be problems the patient will need to attend to at some future time. Carl had come into therapy just out of college. He was excruciatingly anxious and was feeling lost and isolated. Out on his own, he missed the structure of college life. While in school, he had drifted, choosing liberal arts subjects that were gratifying but not connected to any particular goal. He felt unconnected, had few friends, no important relationships with women, and no sense of what he wanted for himself. In his relationships with women, he had been excessively compliant. He was uncomfortable with peers and particularly with "macho" or athletic men.

Carl had worked productively first in individual and then in combined therapy. He had confronted serious relationship issues and understood the origins of some of those problems in terms of his early intense attachment to a very powerful and adoring mother. In the course of therapy Carl had come to choose work that interested him. He had made significant advances in his career and was beginning to feel strong and successful. Recently he had met a young woman and had fallen in love. They had decided to live together. This relationship was different from previous ones, evidencing the changes he had made. He was able to be with a woman, feel close and loving, and at the same time not merge with her as he had done previously.

Carl felt that his work in the group had helped him counter his compliance with strong women and his isolation. Although he was aware of possible problems in his new relationship, he felt ready to leave therapy. It was important for Carl to make his own decision about leaving. He had indeed achieved many of the goals he had set for himself, understood the origins and meanings of his passive behavior, and could identify when he adopted that behavior as a defensive stance.

Here again the group had to work with their own fantasied expectations of perfection for themselves and others. They also had to recognize their transference wishes that the therapist be omnipotent and able to effect magical transformations. Carl was able to acknowledge where he might have problems in the future and to suggest that perhaps someday he would be ready to work on other aspects of his life.

After One Group Member Leaves

When a group member leaves, the group deals with its loss. Although some of the literature has compared the period after a member leaves a group to mourning, this is not necessarily the case. When the termination has been a planned one and when, as in the case of Anthony, the group members have a sense of successful completion, it has been our experience that this is not a period of mourning. There is a palpable sense of loss which can foster a reexamination of the issues surrounding separation and individuation. Many of these feelings are experienced in terms of shifts in the transference.

It is important for the group to have adequate time to deal with all of its feelings about a group member's departure before a new person is introduced to the group. There are times when the most recent member of the group will be particularly involved with this. In anticipation of someone new coming into the group, the recent member will be able to talk about how it felt to be the newcomer, the stranger.

Relationships among group members shift as the group composition changes. Walter and Tom formed a different relationship and worked with each other in new ways after Anthony left the group.

Other Models of Termination

Although we have talked here of a termination model based on ending individual therapy while the patient is still in group and then finally terminating group therapy, this is not the only model.

Occasionally it is appropriate for the patient to leave both individual and group therapy at the same time. When the patient has completed the work of therapy and it is clear there are no problems with separation, it is not appropriate to continue work in group. Just as we indicated earlier, that not all patients should be in group, there are individual differences in how long any particular patient should be in combined therapy or in group therapy.

It is much less usual for patients to leave group and continue in individual therapy for a short while before finally terminating.

There are also instances when individual therapy is terminated before the patient has worked in combined therapy, even though both patient and therapist agree it would be a useful experience. Although combined therapy might be useful to a patient for all the reasons put forth earlier, the circumstances of his or her life may make this choice unwise. For example, Erich had just won custody of his two children after a long and trying legal procedure. He was able to schedule his individual therapy sessions during the day, but felt that during the initial period of readjustment it was more important for him to be at home with his children during the evenings. Since the therapist was aware of how chaotic life had been for these youngsters, she felt that Erich's choice was a wise one. His therapy was eventually terminated without work in combined therapy. Both Erich and his therapist were aware that he had given up work that might have been helpful to him, but it had been important to acknowledge the pressing realities of his life.

Summary

Termination in combined analytic therapy provides an extended stage on which to work out the various aspects of separation and individuation, and of loss and continuity that are part of the process of growth in all stages of life. The ability to sustain loss and retain a cohesive sense of one's self is an important part of this process in therapy. It involves an acknowledgment of the real losses as well as a careful working through of the fantasies and transference distortions evoked by an experience of separation. It also requires a willingness to give up any fantasies of perfection on the part of the patient and the therapist. This is a complex process which takes time. Combined analytic therapy allows the time and provides a context for a full exploration.

C H A P T E R   7

Individual and Group Therapy: Suggestions for Training

I N PRESENTING the material in this volume we have tried to address the range of therapists who might find it valuable to add combined analytic treatment to their practice. That range would include analytically trained therapists with no group experience, and those who have had some experience with group but not specifically with combined treatment. There will be considerable variation in the needs for training or supervision in these groups and each individual will need to tailor a program to his own needs. In this chapter we will present some guidelines we have arrived at from our own experience with training and supervision for combined therapy.

First, no matter how well trained and experienced a practitioner is in individual psychoanalytic treatment, he or she should not try combined treatment until something has been learned about group, experientially as well as cognitively.

When Irving Yalom was writing about training for group therapy in 1975, he deplored the assumption that while specific training was required to do individual therapy, there was no similar conviction about training for doing group therapy. He went on to comment on attempts to correct this which were then taking place. We find that in 1984 the attempts continue, though they seem to have lagged most in psychoanalytic training centers. This, despite the fact that many graduating from these institutes ultimately use group therapy in either private practice or in hospitals and clinics they often head. Frequently there is the assumption that a well-trained psychoanalyst can be an effective group therapist without additional training. However this assumption is frequently unwarranted. Experiences reported by therapists doing group therapy without training, and by patients and administrators of training centers, demonstrate repeatedly that the experience of participating in a group is an essential prerequisite for doing group therapy in general. This is particularly so when doing combined analytic therapy.

Group Experience

Understanding what it feels like to be a member of a group, subject to its dynamics, and learning what one may unconsciously communicate to a group, cannot be experienced without actual participation in one. This experience may be gained in a group with peers or in a therapy group as a patient.

An interesting demonstration of the value of group experience at the most advanced levels of analytic training occurred in a group of analytic therapists within a training institution.

Suggestions for Training

The group was working together on analytic issues in therapy situations involving racial or ethnic differences. It had been agreed that though substantive issues affecting planning the workshop would be addressed, there would be a concerted effort to use the meetings experientially, attending to therapeutic process as well. All of the members of the group had been through psychoanalytic training. There were broad differences, however, in levels of experience and status within the group. In the course of working, Dr. Lorry, a black analyst with extended experience with interracial situations, had emerged as a natural leader. Group members frequently turned to him as an authority or an arbiter of differences.

At one session a new staff member entered the working group. To orient the new person Dr. Lorry made a statement concerning the focus of a planned observation group. He felt that the plan in the group should be to stay with ethnic issues and not get into underlying personal dynamics. The new member asserted unequivocal disagreement with Dr. Lorry's position, feeling that the group would be effective only if underlying individual dynamics were also explored. This led to varied reactions within the group, as some agreed with Dr. Lorry, some with the new member, and some with intermediate positions.

In the following meeting two other members of the group, a man and woman, and both experienced analysts, each talked of feeling personally diminished in previous meetings in interaction with Dr. Lorry. They had each felt unnaturally intimidated and inarticulate in reaction to exchanges with him. In one of the meetings Dr. Stanton, a white male analyst, had volunteered the information that no black patients came to him for treatment and he didn't understand why. Dr. Lorry had queried him about what he did when talking on the phone. Dr. Stanton had not said anything further at the meeting, but after he left had found himself feeling oddly young and inexperienced, and somehow put down. Only afterward did he realize that he had withdrawn, feeling unable to respond. Dr. Stein, the woman analyst, had felt wounded by a casual remark from Dr. Lorry about middle-class liberals. She had not mentioned it until this moment in group. Both she and Dr. Stanton had put aside their reactions, dismissing them as idiosyncratic in contrast to the good colleaguial exchanges they had had with Dr. Lorry in the past, and therefore not worth mentioning.

The group first had to get beyond the complex of racial and ethnic issues involved. Then Dr. Stanton talked of his own history of diffidence and withdrawal in response to authoritative people who reminded him of his powerful mother. Dr. Stein recalled vulnerability to a devastatingly critical father she had learned to tune out. But the response of both analysts had been elicited by a subtly authoritarian position Dr. Lorry had assumed that tended to intimidate them. It could discourage open responsiveness as it left the other person feeling somehow diminished.

Dr. Lorry listened attentively to Dr. Stein and Dr. Stanton. At first he seemed surprised, then taken aback. Then he started to talk about how he had felt in the group and connected this with a defensive stance he had learned very early in life to ward off feeling anxious and threatened. He was able to trace the happenings in the group that had set his defensive behavior off and to acknowledge that he had heard, but had not necessarily attended to comments like this from his family and co-workers.

Subsequent sessions provided the opportunity to attend to Dr. Lorry's defensive stance and the reactions of the other group members to it. Each had the chance to learn more about handling their reactions and modulating them in their roles as group therapists. Dr. Lorry's continued interaction in the group gave him the chance to learn more about handling his own defensive reaction and to modulate it better in the group. In the observation group he was to lead, his defensive stance would have appeared and probably would have gone unmentioned but not consciously unnoticed, which would have affected the group dynamics. This kind of attitude can remain subtly embedded, restricted to never coming out into the open except in a group experience.

There are a broad range of group experiences available for analysts. An advanced and experienced therapist might find peer group experiences the most appropriate and productive. A first experience in group is sometimes easiest at extended psychoanalytic conferences. These settings can provide more anonymity for the therapist who is reluctant to expose inexperience with group or cautious about revealing personal issues in the community or training center within which he or she maintains a senior position. The American Group Psychotherapy Association, meeting in different cities each year, has intensive two- or three-day group experiences at its annual training institutes. The group therapy training department at the Postgraduate Center for Mental Health in New York City has an annual three-day workshop for therapists that provides intensive small group experience with experienced group therapists as leaders. The effectiveness of this kind of experience is seen by the number of experienced group therapists who frequently return for these workshops.

A group experience is a way of combining didactic learning and direct involvement in group dynamics. Feedback from colleagues and the development of cognitive understanding are combined. Each individual participant is able to get a sense of the ways in which they function in a group, some of which may be unique to the group setting. An ongoing group experience, extending over several days or weeks, is a useful bridge between the kinds of self-awareness developed in group therapy and purely theoretical learning. Using data produced in the group for both personal growth and an understanding of group process provide a rich learning experience.

An example of this is seen from an excerpt from the second session of a group experience for advanced students who had completed their training in individual therapy. Bill, a member of the group, announced that things were moving for him professionally. His private practice had expanded and he would be taking on a more central role in the clinic. This led other group members to talk about their professional goals, why they were pursuing further training in groups, and what they saw as their present professional status. As time went on, Francine became agitated and turned to Len, another group member, and spoke contemptuously about how satisfied he seemed with himself, even though to her he didn't seem to be going anywhere in his professional life. Len wondered what Francine was getting so worked up about. Was she asking him to do things she wished she could do? He was feeling quite comfortable and satisfied with what he was doing. As Francine went on to assault Len further, other group members began to see that she was attacking Len for something she couldn't stand in herself and several admitted to similar behaviors in themselves. Francine began to agree that projective identification was involved. The group leader then suggested that perhaps she was feeling competitive with Bill and that this had set her off. The leader encouraged Francine to turn to Bill and talk directly to him. Francine was calmer and more in touch with her feelings as she turned to Bill. She said, "I am angry at myself. I wish I could be like you, you're doing what you want, on your own and respected." Francine then turned abruptly to the leader and exclaimed, "Oh, my God! I just recalled a thought I had about you in the car going home after last week's group. I thought, he is my age and *he* is teaching *us*. I realized how envious I am of you. I wish I could be doing what you are doing. I compare myself with you because we're the same age. I can't believe how that thought came back to me when you asked me to talk to Bill."

The surfacing of Francine's envy and competition in relation to her peers encouraged other members to talk of similar feelings they had experienced. They were able to clarify some of their own defensive maneuvers, denying, avoiding, or acting out on competitive feelings. The leader pointed out that in a group it was common for intense reactions to the therapist to be expressed and enacted in relation to another member, avoiding the dangerous direct confrontation with the leader.

The Therapist as Patient in a Group

For those who can manage it, at least a year's experience in an analytically oriented therapy group is extremely valuable, both for touching on unresolved personal issues and for training.

An issue that has been much debated is whether a group entered into for training should consist entirely of mental health professionals. Our experience has been that the most productive and full experience seems to be in a mixed group of mental health professionals and people from other fields. However, both the therapist and the professional member must attend to the issues carefully to avoid having the professional member use his or her training defensively, becoming an "assistant therapist," or intellectualizing problems.

In a mixed group, there is an extra burden for the mental health professional in acknowledging confusion, gross immaturity in a particular area, or perverse sexuality. The relationship of these issues to functioning and maintaining self-esteem as a mental health professional makes them additionally uncomfortable for a therapist to admit. However, the closer therapists get to addressing their own personal issues in a group, the more likely they are to have a real comprehension of the experience of their patients in a group.

An Analogue of Combined Therapy

For the therapist who is at earlier stages of his training and in the end stages of treatment with an analyst, entry into a group with the same analyst would be best. With combined treatment, as with all forms of analytic therapy, direct experience as a patient is the ideal. For many this is not possible because they have completed individual analysis many years before, or because their individual analysts do not do group therapy. For these people an analogue of combined therapy is to be considered. An approximation of combined therapy can be had by arranging to have a sequence of individual sessions with an analytic group therapist prior to entering the group. The individual sessions would focus on current unresolved issues (certainly some remain even after the most successful treatment); a review of the trainee's understanding of his or her own history and analysis, with particular emphasis on what the analyst meant to the trainee; how the trainee was affected by the relationship; and what the relationship changed for him. This process requires active participation by the new therapist, who exercises a freedom to move into areas where conflict is sensed or a heightening of anxiety perceived.

The issues of interaction, real or fantasied, with the previous therapist and how they impinge on the current therapeutic interaction are particularly important to consider. Comments that may indicate idealization should be questioned and responded to. For example, "He always knew exactly what was going on for me way before I could," or "Bringing dreams to him was marvelous, it was always so simple and apparent to him." The therapist might ask whether there had ever been an exception to this, whether the trainee had ever experienced any disappointment or moment of disillusionment. In some cases the current therapist might offer some realistic communication that he did not know the trainee in this way, that he will have to learn about him, and that this might feel disappointing. The trainee is then encouraged to express any similar feelings as they come up in the future either in the individual session or in the group. It is very likely that these individual sessions will stimulate dreams expressing transferential expectations. They will provide invaluable insights to the form the present relationship is taking. The transference developing with the new therapist will become clear in relation to the described historical patterns.

A family drawing may be requested after four or five sessions. As discussed previously, these are valuable in formulating the patient's present view of his or her development and with it an awareness of remaining defensiveness.

From the outset, the training analyst should make it clear that the relationship which develops during this period of individual sessions is very important to proceeding into the group, and that unless the process evokes confidence and some engagement, it is not wise to go into group with *this* therapist. For many trainee-practitioners this is the first time in years that they are in the position of patient. It enables them to recall some of the forms in which transferential feelings are immediately induced: the feelings of helplessness and vulnerability; the idealization of the therapist with exaggerated expectations; and emotional preoccupation with the therapist's reactions.

Entering into a group that includes a majority of patients in combined treatment is a unique learning experience. One therapist, Dr. Evans, who had already had individual treatment and some group therapy, entered a group as part of her training. The treating therapist worked primarily with combined analytic therapy. Dr. Evans had five sessions before entering group to deal with the issues described above. Her initial entry into the group was simple. She had looked forward to being in a group with a therapist she had chosen and brought in a dream to the first session about going to a lovely, sunny, outdoor gathering. She was experienced with group and knew what her concerns were. However, as the sessions went on, Dr. Evans became more anxious, uncomfortable, and defensive as she permitted herself to experience the subtleties of interactions in the group climate. She realized that she felt as if she were in the midst of a family where she was the only one who didn't belong. Partly this was the imprint of being an only child, but she was also responding to the particular climate in a combined therapy group where the relationship of members reflects a shared history and familiarity with the therapist. This differentiated Dr. Evans from the others and served to redefine her own transferential issues, but it also provided an opportunity to learn firsthand from peers about their experience with combined treatment.

Observation of Group Therapy

Where there is an opportunity to observe an ongoing therapy group (as from a one-way vision room), this, too, can be an important part of training. The opportunity to discuss with a more experienced group therapist what was observed, and why the therapist did what he or she did can be very valuable. This is a unique way to share experiences and learn. Exposure to a variety of practitioners helps a student become aware of differences in each person's way of conducting combined therapy, as well as of the communalities in practice of experienced therapists. The therapist who is beginning the practice of combined therapy can feel free to develop a form consistent with his individual analytic practice.

Watching another therapist gives the trainee the opportunity to gain perspective on the assumptions underlying his or her own analytic practice. What is the quality of the analytic relationships the therapist forms? Does the therapist strive to maintain analytic neutrality? How actively does the therapist work with the transference? With dreams? With history? And do each of these seem to effect change?

We should add that being observed and having an opportunity to discuss what was seen with colleagues is a valuable learning experience for the observed therapist.

Theory and Didactic Education

While we have emphasized the importance of working as a patient, as a participant in a group experience, and as an observer of group therapy practice, other forms of learning are also valuable. Reading and discussion of the literature on group therapy, group dynamics, and group process are all important. The opportunity to relate theory to clinical practice enhances trainees' understanding of both and sharpens their awareness of what they are doing as they begin to work with analytic therapy groups.

Supervision and Consultation

Our experience has shown that supervision—the careful examination of clinical practice by more experienced colleagues—is useful. When one begins to do combined analytic therapy, both individual and group supervision contribute differently to the learning experience.

INDIVIDUAL SUPERVISION

Many of the issues raised by the transition from individual analysis to combined treatment are best dealt with in individual supervisory sessions. In these there is the time and opportunity to examine the individual patient's preparation for reactions in the group. The therapist's new experiences in dealing with his or her individual patients in a group can be best examined in this context.

The period of transition from individual to combined therapy practice may be filled with turmoil for the therapist as well as for the patients. Reverberations from the group back to the individual therapy sessions can be disquieting for everyone. The therapist may have to reevaluate what he or she is doing and, at the very least, deal with his or her anxieties.

In individual supervision questions of which patients to put into group and when are considered. The therapist new to group is sometimes overenthusiastic and may overestimate what group will resolve for a particular patient. This can result in rushing patients into group prematurely or at an inopportune moment in terms of resistance. All the considerations discussed in this volume are relevant and important to maintain so that the therapist does not disrupt his total practice. Therapists coming for consultation after they have gotten into dilemmas frequently feel overwhelmed and that there is no way back. It is certainly preferable that these problems be anticipated in supervision.

The work of Dr. West is an example of how the problems of beginning a group and the effects of combined therapy may be anticipated and worked on in supervision. An experienced analyst, Dr. West was interested in starting a group. She had a number of patients in individual therapy who she felt would profit from group therapy. She herself had been a patient in combined therapy early in her career and was in a group therapy training program. Ready to start her own group, she sought consultation regarding which of her patients could benefit from entering a group.

In individual supervision Dr. West presented the patients she thought might work well together in a group. The dynamics of each patient were discussed, their history, and the nature of their transference at this time in therapy was considered. For example, Anne, a woman in her late thirties, had been in treatment for several years. She had first come into therapy after she divorced her husband, needing to confront her problems with dependency. She had since remarried, had a successful career, and was concerned with the demands of her newly reconstructed family. Initially she had a strong, positive transference to Dr. West. As many of the dependency issues were explored, Anne's ambivalence toward her mother emerged. With this, more anger was expressed toward Dr. West. This had been explored in the middle stages of the individual therapy. At present, though Anne's career was developing, she had problems asserting her authority with people who worked for her. Though she understood some of the underlying issues, she could not make the changes in behavior that would result in easier relationships at work.

Dr. West suggested that a group would provide Anne with the opportunity to further work through her problems of separation and individuation. Her problems in finding appropriate styles of self-assertion and exercise of authority were important. Dr. West was sure that in the protective setting of the dyadic relationship she did not really experience with Anne the ways in which she was offensive to her co-workers and subordinates. Dr. West and Anne were only able to deduce that this was so because of the responses of others to Anne. In the dyadic relationship the transferential responses of hostile dependency had been addressed, but further working through was needed.

Betty had been in therapy for only a year-and-a-half. A young woman in her twenties, she had recently married and was struggling with the conflicts about leaving her parents. They had been divorced when she was in college and she felt needed by each of them. Betty, too, was dealing with issues of separation and individuation. Dr. West and her supervisor felt group to be particularly helpful in working through these problems. For Betty, they thought that expanding the dyadic relationship and working in a group with both men and women of varying ages would be useful.

Dr. West and her supervisor examined the dynamics and the developmental histories of each of these women and anticipated some of the reactions that could be expected in group. Both women had experienced intense rivalry with a younger sibling—Anne with a sister, and Betty with a brother. Both women felt they were very special and needed by their mothers, issues they had become more fully aware of in individual therapy. Though these issues had been worked with there, predictably they would reemerge with more immediacy in the group, which would promote further working through.

Anne and Betty's hypersensitivity to sharing and their attitudes toward Dr. West would certainly be more sharply experienced in the group. It also could be anticipated that the two women would differ in their reactions to the men in the group. Anne had shared her mother's disdain for her father. Betty had felt tied to her mother, but also felt the need to be protective of her father. Dr. West, recalling her own experience in combined analytic therapy and how group therapy had furthered the working through process, felt that Anne and Betty would benefit from combined treatment. The supervisor validated her choices.

Dr. West was also considering two men for the group. David was in his twenties, uncertain about his career goals, and unable to make a commitment to the woman he lived with. She was older, and David had enjoyed being a "father" to her three children. He had begun to explore the meaning of this relationship in therapy, and to understand what he had unconsciously tried to reconstruct for himself in his new family. His initial transference reactions to Dr. West had been negative and adversarial, and he had been suspicious of her interventions. Following that he had allowed himself to acknowledge his more positive feelings and his fears of dependency.

Dr. West felt that there had been significant work done with David's transference reactions in his individual therapy. Both she and the supervisor also felt that working in a group with both men and women would give David the opportunity to reexperience and confront some of his defensive attitudes toward men. He was usually able to get along well with women; as a social worker he was frequently placed in a position in which he was the only man with a group of women.

Karl, in his late forties, had been in individual therapy for a long time and had somehow resisted two attempts to move toward termination. Residual anxieties connected to early abandonment remained operative. Karl often attempted to treat Dr. West as he had his young adult daughters, protective but demeaning, flirtatious, and at the same time very critical. Though these transference reactions had been explored, it was felt that there was still more work needed. Participating in a group would help him proceed further on these issues and manage termination more comfortably.

The complementarity and the different dynamics of the four patients were discussed in detail. It was possible to anticipate how each would react in the transition period from individual to combined treatment. Their responses to the disruption of the dyadic relationship were considered. The clinical experience of the supervisor was helpful to Dr. West as she dealt with the differing responses to moving to combined treatment. The goals for each patient in group therapy were explored; the various levels of the interrelated dynamics were considered.

Dr. West and her supervisor considered other patients for the group. Evelyn was a single parent, living alone with four children but very enmeshed with her mother and sister. Though very different in socioeconomic status from the other four, her dynamic struggles were similar to the others. She was intelligent and insightful. Her early family background was like David's, though he had moved into the professional world. Evelyn had worked with Dr. West for a number of years, and both positive and negative transference issues had been confronted. She was very eager to work in a group and was feeling the need for feedback from peers. It was decided that she enter.

Gloria was another group candidate. She was a younger woman, who had begun therapy with Dr. West only six months ago. She had just started graduate school and was beginning a new relationship with a young man she had recently met. It was decided that it was too early in Gloria's treatment to add group to the individual therapy, especially as she was coping with so many other beginnings.

Two other patients were considered then rejected for group. One, a severely narcissistic young man, had just suffered a serious loss and was not ready to work in a group, needing the support of the dyadic relationship. The other, an older woman, was not yet ready to work in a group because of her inability to tolerate any attention to the needs of others.

The group started with Anne, Betty, David, Karl, and Evelyn. It was assumed that other patients would be added in time. In individual supervision Dr. West was able to discuss the impact of the group on the individual therapy of each of the group members. The effects of the group on individual transferences were noted. The intense rivalry expressed between David and Karl for each of the women, and the intensity of Anne's disdainful responses to Betty, surprised Dr. West. In the supervision, her reactions and countertransferences were explored.

The detailed and careful exploration of the interplay between the group therapy sessions and the individual therapy sessions for each of the five patients comprised the primary focus in the individual supervision that continued for most of the next year.

Group supervision is different than individual and has its own special value. It is often helpful in detecting the therapist's countertransferences and the effects they induce in the group. The likelihood is that the therapist will induce similar feelings in the supervisory group. When the therapist in training discusses impasses with patients in his or her group in a supervisory group, the connections become apparent and are experienced very directly.

Sometimes it is possible to combine group supervision and group experience and this may be an economical solution to problems of obtaining optimal training experiences. An ongoing supervisory group soon learns the character structure and the salient vulnerable issues for each of its members. Examples are the tendency to deny or avoid anger in the group; the subtle preference for a particular kind of person with the reciprocal distancing from others; or the overprotectiveness which leads to too much intervening too soon.

The opportunity to share with peers in an atmosphere of trust and understanding can enhance personal growth and modify professional defensiveness. Supervisory groups, like therapy groups, have to be assembled with awareness of and attention to the needs of the individuals who make up the group.

When Dr. Fox brought her problems with her group to group supervision for consideration, her colleagues listened with concern. They knew her group, as she had discussed them before. They also knew Dr. Fox, having worked together with her for a year. She was concerned that her group seemed to have lost whatever sense of cohesiveness they had had, that they each related to her but not to each other. When one person talked, one man looked out the window, another seemed to be lost in his own thoughts, a woman sat rearranging her clothes and her hair. The interactions between group members had diminished; they now each talked to Dr. Fox alone. As Dr. Fox described the situation to the supervisory group, her voice dragged a bit and group members found themselves inattentive, drifting off in their own thoughts. One of the group members brought up Dr. Fox's recent visit to her family and her sadness that they no longer needed her as they had in the past, and wondered whether the shift in her group could be related to this. The supervisory group was able to help Dr. Fox become aware of her transference reactions to the group, and of the subtle ways in which her own mood shifts had affected her work with them. Without being aware of it, she had stopped encouraging group interactions that did not include her directly.

In another supervisory group, Dr. Black discussed the resistances she was encountering in the group she had just formed. As her colleagues made various suggestions, she responded each time with "Yes, but. . . ." After several repetitions of this, one of the supervisory group members was able to observe that Dr. Black was repeating the behavior of her patients. The group then worked with this example of parallel process and was able to observe the ways in which this had occurred for each of them. They were also able to discuss some of the difficulties in presenting their new groups when they were so anxious as beginning group therapists. Issues of trust in the beginning supervisory group parallel the issues of trust in their newly formed therapy groups.

Dr. Jones was working with a group that had several individuals who had problems with impulse control and had found himself feeling anxious prior to each session. The other members of the supervisory group were able to share their anxieties about working with very angry individuals in their groups. It differed from their work in individual therapy because angry responses can be amplified in group. They compared the methods they had developed to deal with outbursts in their groups, and each was able to consider their individual styles and why they worked as they did. Some found they tried to exclude provocative people from their groups. Others examined their own defensive styles when faced with a patient's explosive rage: some became peacemakers, others sarcastic, some stepped in immediately, others waited too long. The group found this exploration of their countertransference reactions to be useful.

Supervision, whether it is individual or group, facilitates the integration of others' experience but allows for the definition of one's personal style of carrying out the therapeutic tasks. For all of us working with the complexities of combining individual and group therapy, there are a variety of ways in which we can sharpen our clinical perceptions and our therapeutic skills. As supervisors we find we constantly learn from our supervisees. The goal of supervision is not to imitate but to help therapists develop their own skills, understand their own style of working, and sharpen their clinical perceptions.

A Final Note

In general, we advise thoughtful preparation for starting combined treatment in an individual analytic practice. Without planning an entire practice can be considerably disrupted. But with preparation, the addition of group to an individual therapy practice can enhance and enrich the therapeutic process, observably extending changes in each patient who participates.

REFERENCES

Alexander, F. 1961. A metapsychological description of the process of cure —1925. In *The scope of psychoanalysis: selected papers of Franz Alexander 1921–1961.* New York: Basic Books. pp. 205–224.

Appelbaum, S.A. 1981. *Effecting change in psychotherapy.* New York: Jason Aronson. pp. 25–58.

Aronson, M. 1979. The working alliance in combined individual and group psychotherapy. In L. Wolberg and M. Aronson, eds. *Group therapy: 1979.* New York: Stratton International Medical Book Corporation. pp. 10–23.

Aronson, M., Caligor, J., Fried, E., Fieldsteel, N., Liff, Z., Rabin, H., Thorne, R. and Youcha, I. 1976. Unpublished panel presentation. Postgraduate Center for Mental Health, New York, New York.

Bergmann, M. 1966. The intrapsychic and communicative aspects of the dream. *International Journal of Psychoanalysis* 47:356–363.

Bieber, T.B. 1971. Combined individual and group psychotherapy. In H.I. Kaplan and B.J. Sadock, eds. *Comprehensive group psychotherapy.* Baltimore: Williams & Wilkins. pp. 153–69.

Bion, W.R. 1961. *Experience in groups.* New York: Basic Books.

Caligor, J. 1980. The analytic therapist in the group 1980: Continuities and discontinuities with Sigmund Freud. *Group* 4:32–39.

Caligor, L., and May, R. 1968. *Dreams as symbols: Man's unconscious language.* New York: Basic Books.

Cartwright D., and Zander, A. 1968. *Group Dynamics.* New York: Harper & Row.

De Rosis, L. 1975. Karen Horney's theory applied to psychoanalysis in groups. In Rosenbaum, M., and Berger, M., eds. *Group psychotherapy and group function.* New York: Basic Books. pp. 215–43.

Dewald, P.A. 1982. The clinical importance of the termination phase. *Psychoanalytic Inquiry* 3:441–62.

Durkin, H. 1962. *The group in depth.* New York: International Universities Press. p. 140.

Dyrud, J. 1980. Remembrance of things past and present. *Contemporary Psychoanalysis* 16:335–47.

Erikson, E. 1950. *Childhood and society.* New York: W.W. Norton.

References

Fenichel, O. 1976. Concerning the theory of psychoanalytic technique. In M.S. Bergmann and F. R. Hartman, eds. *The evolution of psychoanalytic techniques.* New York: Basic Books. p. 463.

Ferenczi, S. 1955 (orig. 1930). The principle of relaxation and neocatharsis. In M. Balint, ed. *Final contributions to the problems and methods of psychoanalysis.* New York: Basic Books. pp. 108–125.

Firestein, S.K. 1978. *Termination in psychoanalysis.* New York: International Universities Press.

Foulkes, S.H., and Anthony, E.J., eds. 1957. *Group psychotherapy: The psychoanalytic approach.* Harmondsworth, England: Penguin Books.

Freud, S. 1953 (orig. 1900). *The interpretation of dreams.* Standard Edition (hereafter: S.E.), Vols. IV and V. London: The Hogarth Press.

———. 1958 (orig. 1914). Remembering, repeating and working through. In S.E., Vol. XII. pp. 145–56.

———. 1955 (orig. 1921). Group psychology and the analysis of the ego. In S.E., Vol. XVIII. pp. 67–143.

———. 1961 (orig. 1916–1917). Introductory lectures on psychoanalysis. In S.E., Vol. XV. Parts 1 & 2, pp. 15–239. In S.E. 1963 Vol. XVI. Part 3, pp. 243–463.

Gedo, J.E. 1979. Beyond interpretation: Toward a revised theory for psychoanalysis. New York: International Universities Press.

———. 1981. Advances in clinical psychoanalysis. New York: International Universities Press.

Glatzer, H.T. 1959. Notes on the pre-oedipal fantasy. *American Journal of Orthopsychiatry* 29:383–390.

———. 1962. Handling narcissistic problems in group therapy. *International Journal of Group Psychotherapy* 12:448–455.

Greenson, R. 1967. *The technique and practice of psychoanalysis.* New York: International Universities Press.

Heider, F. 1958. *The psychology of interpersonal relations.* New York: John Wiley and Sons.

Horney, K. 1953. *New ways in psychoanalysis.* New York: W.W. Norton.

Jones, E.E., and Davis, K. E. 1965. From acts to dispositions. In L. Berkowitz, ed. *Advances in experimental social psychology.* Vol. 2. New York: Academic Press.

Kadis, A. 1956. Reexperiencing the family constellation in group psychotherapy. *Journal of Individual Psychology* 1:63–68.

———. 1957. Early childhood recollections as aids in group psychotherapy. *Journal of Individual Psychology* 3:182–87.

Kardiner, A. 1939. *The individual and his society.* New York: Columbia University Press.

References

————. 1945. *The psychological frontiers of society*. New York: Columbia University Press.

Karush, A. 1967. Working through: Its widening scope and some aspects of metapsychology. *Psychoanalytic Quarterly* 4:497–531.

Kelley, H.H. 1967. Attribution theory in social science. In D. Levine, ed. *Nebraska symposium on motivation*. Omaha: University of Nebraska Press. pp. 192–238.

Kernberg, O. 1976. *Object relations theory and clinical psychoanalysis*. New York: Jason Aronson.

Kohut, H. 1977. *The restoration of the self*. New York: International Universities Press.

Klein, M. 1975. Notes on some schizoid mechanisms. In M. Klein, ed. *Envy and gratitude and other works, 1946–1983*. New York: Delacorte Press. pp. 1–24.

Klein-Lipschutz, E. 1953. Comparison of dreams in individual and group psychotherapy. *International Journal of Group Psychotherapy* 3:143–49.

Levenson, E. 1972. *The fallacy of understanding*. New York: Basic Books.

Lewin, K. 1951. *Field theory in social science*. New York: Harper Torchbooks.

Lewin, K. 1947. Group decision and social change. In T.M. Newcomb and E.L. Hartley, eds. *Readings in social psychology*. New York: Henry Holt & Co. pp. 197–211.

Lieberman, M.A., Yalom, I., and Miles, M.B. 1973. *Encounter groups: First facts*. New York: Basic Books.

Lippit, R., and White, R.K. 1947. An experimental study of leadership and group life. In T.M. Newcomb and E.L. Hartley, eds. *Readings in social psychology*. New York: Henry Holt & Co. pp. 300–315.

Loewald, H.W. 1960. On the therapeutic action of psychoanalysis. *International Journal of Psychoanalysis* 41:16–33.

Mahler, M., Pine, F., and Bergmann, A. 1975. *The psychological birth of the human infant*. New York: Basic Books.

McDougall, W. 1920. *The group mind*. New York: Putnam Press.

Modell, A.H. 1976. The holding environment and the therapeutic action of psychoanalysis. *Journal of the American Psychoanalytic Association* 24:-285–308.

Ormont, L., and Strean, H. 1978. *The practice of conjoint therapy: Combining individual and group treatment*. New York: Human Sciences Press.

Pratt, J.H. 1907. The class method of treating consumption in the homes of the poor. *Journal of the American Medical Association* 49:755–59.

————. 1975. The tuberculosis class: An experiment in home treatment. In

M. Rosenbaum and M. Berger, eds. *Group psychotherapy and group function.* New York: Basic Books. pp. 131–42.

Racker, H. 1957. The meanings and uses of countertransference. *Psychoanalytic Quarterly* 26:303–57.

Rosenbaum, M., and Berger, M., eds. 1975. *Group psychotherapy and group function.* New York: Basic Books. p. 4.

Schafer, R. 1983. *The analytic attitude.* New York: Basic Books.

Schecter, D.E. 1959. The integration of group theory with individual psychoanalysis. *Psychiatry* 22:267–76.

Searles, H. 1979. *Countertransference and related subjects.* New York: International Universities Press. pp. 172–91.

Silverman, L. 1976. Psychoanalytic theory: "The reports of my death are greatly exaggerated." *American Psychologist* 31:621–37.

Sophocles. 1947. Oedipus the king. In C.T. Murphy et al, eds. *Greek and Roman classics in translation.* New York: Logmans, Green and Co. p. 229.

Spence, D. 1982. *Narrative truth and historical truth: Meaning and interpretation in psychoanalysis.* New York: W.W. Norton.

Stolorow, R., and Lachman, F. 1980. *The psychoanalysis of developmental arrests.* New York: International Universities Press.

Stone, L. 1961. *The psychoanalytic situation.* New York: International Universities Press.

Sullivan, H.S. 1953. *The interpersonal theory of psychiatry.* New York: W.W. Norton.

Wolf, A., and Schwartz, E. 1962. *Psychoanalysis in groups.* New York: Grune & Stratton.

Winnicott, D.W. 1965. *The maturational process and the facilitating environment.* New York: International Universities Press.

———. 1971. *Playing and reality.* New York: Basic Books. pp. 86–94.

Whitaker, D.A. 1976. A group centered approach. *Group Process* 7:37–57.

Yalom, I. 1975. *The theory and practice of group psychotherapy.* New York: Basic Books.

Zajonc, R.B. 1965. Social facilitation. *Science* 149:269–74.

Zajonc, R.B., and Sales, S.M. 1966. Social facilitation of dominant and subordinate responses. *Journal of Experimental Social Psychology* 2:160–68.

INDEX

Acceptance of parents, 125

Acting out, request for group as, 50–52

Adding group, 47–50; emotional responses to, 72–73; family of patient and, 47; quality of working alliance and, 46; *see also* Analytic group

Advantages of individual therapy, 5

Aftermath of termination for analytic group, 182–83

Aggression, group membership and, 39

Alexander, F., 31

Ambivalence, 74, 174–77

Analog of combined therapy, 192–94

Analysts; *see* Therapist(s)

Analytic Attitude, The (Schafer), 12–13

Analytic group, 38–68; acting out in transference and, 50–52; adding to, 47–50, 72–73; alliances within, 58–59; anger expressed in, 115–18; anxiety about entering, 38–40, 75–76; case study, 61–68; climate of, 107–8; composition of, 54–55; conflicts reactivated by, 90–92; confrontation of characterological defenses by, 32–35; criteria for membership, 41–42; defensive behavior elicited by, 4; developmen-

tal theory and transition to, 25–27; dreams in, 153–64; ego strength and, 55; entry during working through, 4–5; entry into, 38–44, 75–76; fantasizing about new member, 88–89; fantasizing entry into, 73–74; impact of leaving member on, 182–83; impact of new member on, 95–97, 142–45; impact on new member, 80–87; impact on transference of, 99–104; individual history and, 52–54; language and mythology of, 59–61; loss of cohesion of, 202–3; narcissism and, 44–46; outside interactions, 57–58; parallel process and, 203; planning termination of member, 173–77; power of, 115–19; preparation for transition, 87–97; primitive emotional processes activated by, 39; resistance in, 119–26; rules of, 56–58; shared universals in, 124–26; starting, 197–201; subgrouping within, 58–59; symbiotic relationships in, 46–47; therapist, relationship with, 55–56; therapist as patient in, 191–92; transference activated by, 30–31, 99–104; transference displaced among, 40–41; transference distortions resolved by, 36–37; vulnerability and, 55; working alliance ex-

Index

Analytic group *(continued)*
tended to, 55–56; working through and, 4–5, 107–8, 153–164

Analytic group therapy, growth of, 5–8

Analytic relationship: combined therapy and, 35–37; disruption of exclusivity of, 79–80; development of, 70; inequality of, 35–37; nonverbal communication, 109–10; roles in, traditional, 122–23; working through and, 106–7

Anger: caused by termination, 174–75; expressed in analytic group, 115–18

Anorexia nervosa, 70–71

Anthony, E.J., 9

Anxiety: about displacement by new group member, 89; about entering group, 38–40, 75–76; about everyday life experiences, 73; about individuation, 65–66; among peers, 52–54; characterological defenses and, 8; dreams, generalized, 76, 151–52; of therapist, 203–4; of transition period, 79–87

Appelbaum, S., 19, 114

Aronson, M., 8

Associations: dream-evoked, 159–60; of therapist to patient's, 122–23

Attitudes toward dreams, 147–49

Autonomy, development of, 32

Berger, M., 6

Bergmann, A., 24–25, 80

Bergmann, M., 148, 171, 172

Bieber, T., 8

Bion, W., 39, 80

Caligor, J., 23

Caligor, L., 148

Cartwright, D., 6

Case studies and examples: of analytic group, 61–68; of analytic group's effect on transference, 99–104; of analytic group's impact on entering patient, 80–87; of analytic group's mythologizing, 60–61; of analytic group's reaction to new member, 95–97, 142–45; of analytic group's routine, 112–19; of anger expressed in group, 115–18; of anxiety about group entry, 75–76; of anxiety among peers, 52–54; of characterological defenses, 33–35; of countertransference-transference deadlock, 99–100; of defensive behavior, 4; of dreams in working through, 161–63; of dream work, 62–64, 65; of "false self," 28–29; of fear of individuation, 65–66, 197–99; of grandiosity, 72; of initiating treatment, 13–15; of life story revision, 16–17; of limitations of individual therapy, 20–23; of mutual attraction of reciprocal character traits, 58–59; of narcissism, 44, 47–50; of neurosis, 43–44; of new member's effect on group, 95–97, 142–45; of only child adding group, 47–50; of par-

Index

Dewald, P.A., 171
Didactic education, 195–96
Displacement, anxiety over, 89
Disruption of symbiotic transference, 46–47
Distortion, inequality of analytic relationship and, 36
Dream(s): in analytic group, 153–63; attitudes toward, 147–49; as communication during working-through, 163–64; during individual phase, 149–51; during transition phase, 151–53; evoked by associations, 159–60; general anxiety, 151–52; as intrapsychic event, 148; manifest content of, 154; material, stimulation for, 94–97; others' reaction to, 159; reporting of, 156–59; as source of self-esteem, 165; symbolization in, 149; transference issues elicited by, 161; transference reactions as manifested in, 157; at transition, 151–53; work, 62–65, 149; in working through, 147–65
Durkin, H., 7–8, 80
Dyadic analytic treatment; see individual therapy
Dynamics, group, 6–7
Dyrud, J., 16

Education, didactic, 195–96
Effectiveness of group therapy on defensive maneuvers, 7–8
Ego development, 18, 19
Ego strength, 55, 76
Ego-syntonic defenses: addressed by

combined therapy, 32–35; anxiety and, 8; "false self," 27–29; narcissism as, 9
Emotional experience, corrective, 31–32
Emotional learning, 109
Emotional processes, primitive, group-activated, 39
Emotional responses to adding group, 72–73
Empathy: individual differences and obstacles to, 54–55; level of integration and, 45–46
Entry into analytic group, 38–44, 75–76
Envy, 174–77
Erikson, E., 35
Examples; see Case studies and examples
Exclusivity of patient-therapist relationship, disruption of, 79–80
Expansion of therapeutic possibilities, 29–31
Experience as participant, 108–9
Exposure of therapist, 108
Extension of working alliance, 55–56

Fallacy of Understanding, The (Levenson), 19
"False self," 27–29
Family: acceptance of, 125; adding group and, 47
Family drawings: assignment of and resistance to, 77–79; use during transition, 76–79

Index

Index

Index

Theory: about narcissism, 44–45; relating to clinical practice, 195–96

Therapeutic needs, variation during treatment process of, 11–12

Therapeutic stance, 29–30

Therapist(s): anxiety of, 203–4; association to patient's story, 122–23; awareness of, 108–9; countertransference of, effect on group, 202–3; exposure of, 108; in group experience, 108–9, 189–91; neutrality of, 29–30; observing other therapists, 195; parallel process of, 203; as patient in analytic group, 191–92; perspectives on transition, 97–104; previous interaction with, 193; relationship with analytic group, 55–56; role in transition, 93–94; "role playing," 108; trainee, 192–94; view on introducing new group member, 92–93; *see also* Training suggestions

Timing of transition, 93–94

Trainees, 192–94

Training suggestions, 185–204; analog of combined therapy, 192–94; consultation, 196–204; group experience, 186–91; observation group therapy, 195; supervision, 196–204; theory and didactic education, 195–96; therapist as patient in analytic group, 191–92

Transferences: acting out in, 50–52; analytic group's effect on, 30–31, 99–104; -countertransference deadlock, 99–100; defined, 15; displaced onto group members, 40–41; distortions, resolution of, 36–37; dream-elicited issues of, 161;

group therapy and quality of, 42–44; in individual therapy, 15; narcissistic, 42–43, 44; negative, 17–18; neurotic, 42, 43–44; reactions as manifested in dreams, 157; request for group and, 50–52; resistance, 51–52; resolution of, 36

Transformation, expectation of, 124–25

Transition, 69–104; anxiety about, 79–87; developmental theory and, 25–27; dreams at, 151–53; family drawings, use of, 76–79; group preparation for, 87–97; initiation of, 69–71; patient's experience and, 79–87; process of, 71–76; regression and, 25–27; therapist's perspective on, 97–104; therapist's role in, 93–94; timing of, 93–94; working alliance and, 92–93

Treatment, initiating, 13–15

"True self," 27–29

Universals, shared, in analytic group, 124–26

Variation in therapeutic needs, 11–12

Views of analytic roles, traditional, 122–23

Vignettes; *see* Case studies and examples

Vulnerability: degree of, group com-

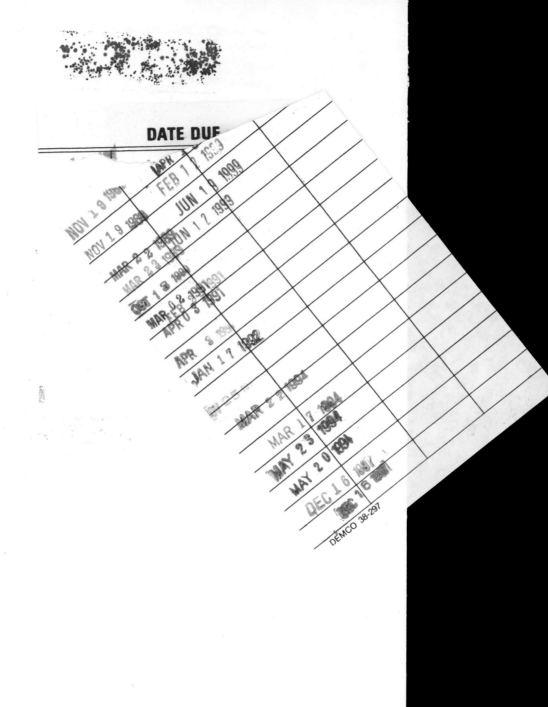